THE LIVING ROOM

TRADITIONAL WOODWORKING

THE LIVING ROOM

Step-by-step projects for the woodworker

Watson-Guptill Publications/New York

First published in the United States by Watson-Guptill Publications,
a division of BPI Communications, Inc.,
1515 Broadway, New York, N. Y. 10036

Originally published by Collins & Brown Ltd,
London House, Great Eastern Wharf,
Parkgate Road, London SW11 4NQ

ISBN 0 8230 5402 0

Library of Congress Catalog Card Number : 97-62557

Series Editor: Liz Dean
Project Editor: Ian Kearey
Editorial Assistant: Lisa Balkwill
Designer: Suzanne Metcalfe-Megginson
Illustrator: Keith Field

Editorial Director: Sarah Hoggett
Art Director: Roger Bristow

Printed in China

First printing, 1998

1 2 3 4 5 6 7 8 9 / 06 05 04 03 02 01 00 99 98

CONTENTS

Introduction 6

THE PROJECTS
LADIES' WRITING DESK 10

CD STORAGE RACK 16

CHERRY BOOKCASE 20

SIDE TABLE 26

OAK COFFEE TABLE 30

DOUBLE DISPLAY SHELF 36

MANTELPIECE 40

INLAID TABLE 46

DRAWER BENCH 52

WINDSOR ARMCHAIR 58

PINE BOOKCASE 66

CLASSIC MIRROR 70

FINISHING
WAX WORKS 74

Index 78
Acknowledgments 80

INTRODUCTION

THE PROFESSIONAL AND amateur furniture makers who designed and created these projects were selected for their classic and timeless designs, high-quality craftsmanship, innovative techniques, and, not least, the ability to explain precisely how their pieces can be made. These inspiring projects reflect a range of woodworking skills, and with their clear and detailed instructions, step-by-step photographs, and color exploded diagrams, they are well within the grasp of all enthusiastic woodworkers.

Many modern furniture styles emulate the fine lines of Sheraton or Regency, the functional grace of Shaker, or the gentle shapes of country-style designs. The Ladies' Writing Desk (p. 10), Cherry Bookcase (p. 20), and Windsor Armchair (p. 58), for example, reflect these ever-popular influences. The intricate techniques that characterize the more advanced pieces – such as basic woodturning and marquetry – are explained within the context of the projects in which they are used. Hints, tips, and variations are also given, so you can adapt an item to suit your skill level and the workshop tools that are available to you.

Tools and Materials

Traditional style does not have to mean traditional methods. We have assumed that the reader has at least some background in handling and using traditional hand tools, and we also know that modern power tools can help save precious time. In many of the projects shown here, the maker has used power tools, reflecting the explosion in the power tool market over the last few decades. However, don't be disheartened if your workshop is not groaning with the latest equipment – practically all of these projects can be made using few power tools, although in many cases a router, jigsaw, and sander can make life easier. Where possible, the maker has suggested hand tools that can be used as alternatives to power tools.

If you are relying upon hand tools only, your basic tool kit should consist of a workbench, basic saws such as the tenon, coping, dovetail, and ripsaw, C and bar clamps, and a number of marking devices such as steel rules, try squares, a mortise gauge, marking knife, and pencil. You will also need access to a selection of planes, chisels, screwdrivers, a hammer, a drill, and some sort of sharpening system. A selection of sandpapers to prepare wood for finishing is also essential.

While many of these projects rely on the maker having some basic skills, there are several projects in this book, such as the Side Table (p. 26), and the Double Display Shelf (p. 36), that the beginner would be able to complete successfully. The detailed instructions give both the novice and the veteran plenty of projects to choose from.

Left: *The clean lines of this writing desk (p. 10) accentuate the simplicity of its classic design.*

All the projects in this book are made from solid softwood or hardwood, either commonly available or imported timber. Again, suggestions are included for alternative woods, leaving you to make an informed choice based on your working preferences, a piece's style, and your budget constraints. It is best to purchase wood from a local lumber yard, which will frequently offer a wider selection than most home improvement stores, and will cut wood to meet your project's specifications.

Finally, consider your project's finish. For best results, you should decide on the finish at the start of a project rather than at the end. There are a great many products available nowadays, from French polish to liming. You will find some guidelines in the instructions for each project, but the choice of finish is ultimately yours. The section on finishing at the end of the book (pp. 74–77) demonstrates how to make and apply a basic wax, and create colored waxes to your taste.

We hope that the projects in this book provide a broad overview of designs and techniques, as well as the inspiration to make and enjoy many of them.

Right: *This pine bookcase (p. 66) is suitable for a beginner woodworker.*

LADIES' WRITING DESK

The elegant design of this writing desk is loosely based on the eighteenth-century Hepplewhite style. It looks particularly good in oak, and can be made largely using portable power tools.

Lap or half-blind dovetail joints are used for the drawer fronts of the desk.

1 Mark and cut the narrow boards for the top to 4 ft 6 in (1371 mm) length and plane the panels along their edges using a jointer plane. Use a biscuit joiner to make slots, insert beech biscuits and glue and clamp the panels together edge to edge, or drill the edges and insert dowels. Round off the corners and mold the edges and corners. Sand the top with 120-grit sandpaper in a belt sander, then finish with an orbital sander and 150-grit paper. Cut the front and back rails to 4 ft 5⅞ in (1366 mm) length.

2 Cut the side rails to 1 ft 5³⁄₁₆ in (438 mm) length, then cut haunched tenons in each end. Drill holes for 1¼ in (32 mm) no. 8 brass screws along the length of the top front rail. Cut a beaded profile on the side and back rails, and a rabbet along the inside faces of the side, back and bottom front rails. Cut the uprights to 3½ in (90 mm) length, and drill a dowel hole in each end. Mark and drill holes in the top and bottom front rails, insert dowels and glue and clamp the front rail assembly.

3 Mark and cut the legs to 2 ft 3½ (700 mm) length, then mark the mortise lengths for the side and back rails around them in pairs. Mark out the mortises, then use a ⁵⁄₁₆ in (8 mm) drill bit to drill out the waste and chop out the rest with a ¼ in (6 mm) bevel-edge chisel. Repeat for the front rails on the inside edges of the front legs. Taper all four legs on their inside faces, leaving the outside faces straight. Mark the gentle taper using a straightedge, starting 5⅛ in (130 mm) from the top of each leg, then clamp each leg in a bench vice and use a jointer plane to form the taper.

4 Mark and cut the three kickers, three runners and three guides to lengths of 1 ft 3½ in (393 mm). Drill two ⁵⁄₁₆ in (8 mm) holes in both ends of the kickers, insert fluted dowels and bore corresponding holes on the rails. Repeat for the runners, using ⅛ in (4 mm) dowel holes, again drilling corresponding holes in the rails. In the top face of the guides, drill a hole at each end and one in the center, to take 1⅛ in (30 mm) no. 8 brass counter-sunk screws, and fix the guides to the runners. Dry-assemble the rails to the legs and glue the end rails to the legs, clamping them with bar clamps.

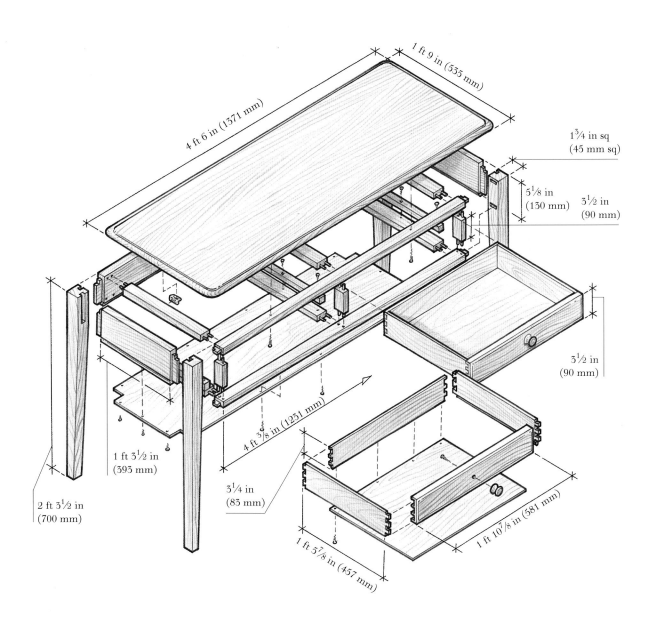

1 ft 9 in (535 mm)

4 ft 6 in (1371 mm)

1¾ in sq (45 mm sq)

5⅛ in (130 mm)

3½ in (90 mm)

3½ in (90 mm)

4 ft 3/8 in (1231 mm)

1 ft 3½ in (393 mm)

3¼ in (83 mm)

2 ft 3½ in (700 mm)

1 ft 5⅞ in (457 mm)

1 ft 10⅞ in (581 mm)

5 Glue and join the front and rear rails to the legs, and the kickers and runner assemblies to the front and rear rails. Check the whole frame and legs for square.

6 Clamp the whole assembly tight with bar clamps, again checking for square. Use a damp rag and an old chisel to wipe and scrape away any excess glue from the joints. Let dry completely.

7 Fix brass right-angled movement stretcher plates to the top inside faces of the back and side rails, attach the top, and insert screws through the holes in the top front rail. Position and glue drawer stops to the top surface of the runners.

8 Cut the drawer sides to 1 ft 5⅞ in (457 mm) and the drawer backs and fronts to 1 ft 10⅞ in (581 mm). Cut ⅛ in (4 mm) grooves ½ in (12 mm) up from the bottom along the sides and fronts, and reduce the bottoms of the backs by ½ in (12 mm) to allow the drawer bottoms to be inserted. Mark and cut lap or half-blind dovetail joints for the fronts and adjoining side ends, and through-dovetails for the backs and adjoining side ends. Glue and clamp the drawer assemblies. Cut drawer bottoms from ⅛ in (4 mm) plywood, and slide into the grooves in the sides and fronts.

9 Fix the drawer bottoms to the underside of the back edges with ¾ in (19 mm) brass woodscrews. Round over the edges of the drawer fronts using an ovolo cutter, and finish the drawers by fixing rounded oak pulls to the fronts. Mark out and cut the panels of ¼ in (6 mm) oak veneered plywood to fit to the underside of the four rails, notching the corners to fit around the tops of the legs. Fix them to the rabbets in the rails, using ¾ in (19 mm) brass woodscrews. Sand the whole table, seal with shellac sealer, and use a clear wax to finish.

LIST OF MATERIALS (*measurements indicate cut size*)

ITEM	SECTION	LENGTH
Hardwood for top, 1	1 ft 9 in x $^7/_8$ in (535 x 21 mm)	4 ft 6 in (1371 mm)
Hardwood for legs, 4	$1^3/_4$ x $1^3/_4$ in (45 x 45 mm)	9 ft 2 in (2800 mm)
Hardwood for front rails, 2	$1^1/_2$ x $^3/_4$ in (38 x 19 mm)	8 ft $11^3/_4$ in (2732 mm)
Hardwood for side and back rails, 3	5 x $^3/_4$ in (125 x 19 mm)	7 ft $4^1/_4$ in (2242 mm)
Hardwood for uprights, 3	$1^5/_8$ x $^3/_8$ in (40 x 10 mm)	$10^1/_2$ in (270 mm)
Hardwood for kickers, 3	$2^1/_4$ x $1^1/_2$ in (55 x 38 mm)	3 ft $10^1/_2$ in (1179 mm)
Hardwood for guides, 3	$^3/_4$ x $^3/_4$ in (19 x 19 mm)	3 ft $10^1/_2$ in (1179 mm)
Hardwood for runners, 3	$1^5/_8$ x $^3/_4$ in (40 x 19 mm)	3 ft $10^1/_2$ in (1179 mm)
Hardwood for drawer fronts, 2, backs, 2, and sides, 4	$3^1/_2$ x $^1/_2$ in (90 x 12 mm)	13 ft 7 in (4152 mm)
Oak veneered plywood for drawer bottoms, 2	1 ft $5^7/_8$ in x $^3/_{16}$ in (457 x 4 mm)	3 ft $10^3/_4$ in (1162 mm)
Oak veneered plywood for dustboard, 1	1 ft $5^5/_{16}$ in x $^1/_4$ (440 x 6 mm)	4 ft $1^1/_2$ in (1256 mm)
Hardwood fluted dowels	$^5/_{16}$ in (8 mm) diameter	
Brass woodscrews	$^3/_4$ in (19 mm) diameter	
Hardwood drawer pulls, 2		
Brass stretcher plates, 6, and beech biscuits		

Working with Oak

Apply wax to the sole of the plane to keep it from shimmying over the grain of the oak; this practice also applies to similar-grain woods. Use a beeswax block or candle wax, and re-apply at intervals. It is best to use brass woodscrews in oak, as steel can stain the wood (see "Finishing Oak," p.33).

CD STORAGE RACK

This space-saving rack can be made from selected hardwood or softwood, or from offcuts of larger projects. It uses a simple notched joint construction to construct a frame for pre-formed plastic CD holders.

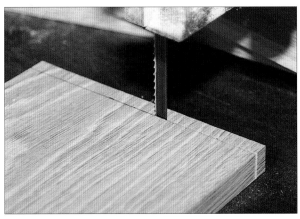

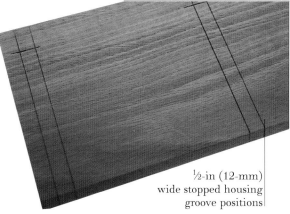

½-in (12-mm) wide stopped housing groove positions

1 Mark and cut the top and bottom to 1 ft 1 in (330 mm), and the sides and middle to 1 ft 6½ in (470 mm). Mark the edges of the top and bottom to take the decorative molding of your choice, and cut it using a router, or mark up and plane a bevel.

2 Mark out the positions of the stopped housing grooves for the sides and middle, from the back of the top and bottom. The side grooves run 5¼ in (133 mm) from the back and the middle 5 in (125 mm). All are ½ in (12 mm) wide. Check that the CD holders will fit inside the spaces.

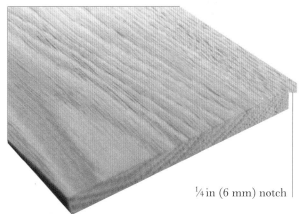

¼ in (6 mm) notch

3 Cut the grooves to a depth of ¼ in (6 mm), using a handsaw or cross-cut power saw, and clean out the waste with a chisel (see inset). Make sure that the depth of each groove is even, and test-fit the sides and middle.

4 Mark and cut a ¼ x ¼ in (6 x 6 mm) notch, ¼ in (6 mm) from the back of the inside edge of each side piece. You can use a ¼ in (6 mm) router cutter, a rip saw, or cut by hand.

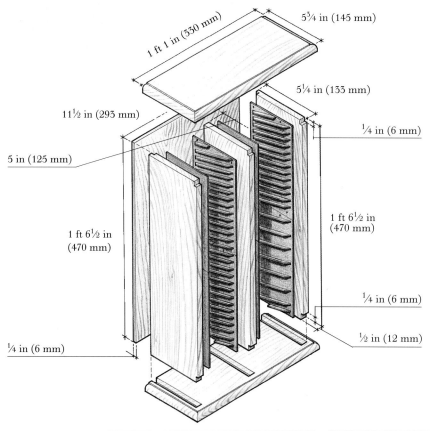

5¾ in (145 mm)

1 ft 1 in (330 mm)

5¼ in (133 mm)

11½ in (293 mm)

¼ in (6 mm)

5 in (125 mm)

1 ft 6½ in
(470 mm)

1 ft 6½ in
(470 mm)

1 ft 6½ in
(470 mm)

¼ in (6 mm)

¼ in (6 mm)

½ in (12 mm)

LIST OF MATERIALS *(measurements indicate cut size)*		
ITEM	**SECTION**	**LENGTH**
Hardwood/softwood for sides, 2	5¼ x ½ in (133 x 12 mm)	3 ft 1 in (940 mm)
Hardwood/softwood for top and bottom, 2	5¾ x ⅝ in (145 x 15 mm)	2 ft 2 in (660 mm)
Hardwood/softwood for middle, 1	5 x ½ in (125 x 12 mm)	1 ft 6½ in (470 mm)
Plywood for back, 1	11½ x ¼ in (293 x 6 mm)	1 ft 6½ in (470 mm)
Panel nails	½ in (12 mm)	
Plastic CD holders and fitting screws		

Choosing CD Holders

The pre-formed black plastic CD holders used here are available in pairs, right- and left-handed. Each single holder takes up to 13 single CDs, and each double holder takes up to six double CDs. Here, two single holders were fitted to the left side of the rack, and one single and one double to the right side. This allows for a maximum of 40 single and seven double CDs. The holders can be cut to fit any installation height, so that the measurements can be varied as necessary. Always purchase the CD holders before you begin the project.

5 First mark then cut a ¼ x ¼ in (6 x 6 mm) notch on the front edges of the sides and middle as shown. Next, test-fit the pieces to the top and bottom. Check that the plastic CD holders fit correctly into the dry assembly.

6 Disassemble the pieces and apply a first coat of varnish, taking care not to cover the joints. Do not coat the inner sides and middle walls, as these will be covered by the plastic CD holders. Sand lightly when dry. Apply PVA glue to the joints and assemble the pieces. Finally, clamp the frame using four bar clamps and let dry completely.

Screw positions for CD holders

7 Apply a second coat of varnish. When this is dry, mark the screw holes for the CD holders on the insides of the sides and the middle wall, and screw them in place. Cut the ¼ in (6 mm) plywood back to 11½ x 1 ft 6½ in (293 x 470 mm) and position on back of frame. Drill nail holes through the back just into the frame and fix the back in place with ½ in (12 mm) panel nails. Apply a coat of varnish to the back.

CHERRY BOOKCASE

This cabinet can be made primarily with portable power tools. It provides
plenty of storage space for all sizes of books, due to its adjustable shelves,
and the cupboard area below keeps items safely out of the way.

1 Mark and cut the top, cupboard top and bottom panels
to 3 ft 1¼ in (945 mm) length, and the side panels to 5 ft
10 in (1780 mm) length. If using several narrow pieces to
make each panel, plane and then slot their edges in stages
to take beech biscuits. Apply glue and clamp up the panels.

2 Sand all panels by hand or using a belt sander and
frame. Mark and cut the front and back top rails to
3 ft 1¼ in (945 mm) length. Draw a template for the front
top rail shape onto ³⁄₁₆ in (4 mm) hardboard, then cut and
use this to cut the shape on the front top rail.

3 Mark and cut ⅜ in (10 mm) rabbets the length of the
back of the top, sides and bottom, to take the bead and
butt boards and the plywood at the back. Mark and cut 1⅛ x
¾ in (30 x 19 mm) stopped rabbets on the front edges of the
top, cupboard top and bottom, for the upright fascias.

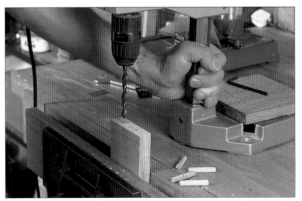

4 Measure and mark out positions for the dowel holes
on the edges of the top, cupboard top, bottom and top
rails, and on inside face of the sides, using dowel pins
where necessary. Drill the holes using a ⁵⁄₁₆ in (8 mm)
drill bit with a pointed spur tip.

5 Use a measuring stick to mark the shelf insert holes on the inside faces of the sides for the top three shelves and pot shelf. Drill the holes using a $\frac{1}{4}$ in (6 mm) drill bit, and tap in shelf inserts and lug supports. Cut all shelves to 3 ft $1\frac{1}{8}$ in (943 mm) length, and plane edges square. Mark and cut the two upright fascia panels to 5 ft 10 in (1780 mm) length, and cut a single beaded profile down the inside faces, using a $\frac{3}{16}$ in (4 mm) single bead router cutter.

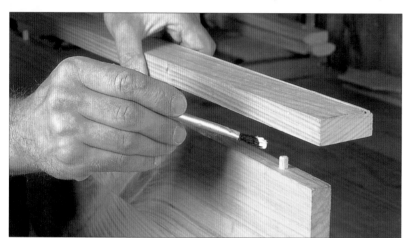

6 Mark and drill $\frac{5}{16}$ in (8 mm) dowel holes in the front edges of the sides and the back of the upright fascias. Next, dry-assemble the top, cupboard top, bottom, sides and top rails, checking that all the joints are snug, then insert all dowels as shown, apply glue and clamp together the whole carcass, checking for square. When dry, insert dowels and apply glue to the upright fascias and front side edges, and clamp together.

7 Mark and cut the door stiles to 2 ft $1\frac{3}{4}$ in (655 mm) length and door rails to 1 ft 3 in (380 mm) length, and cut traditional mortises and tenons. Cut an ovolo molding along both the front face edges of the stiles and rails, and miter near each mortise-and-tenon joint. Cut rabbets to the same depth as the outside molding to the inside back edges of the stiles and rails. Dry-assemble the door frames, checking for square.

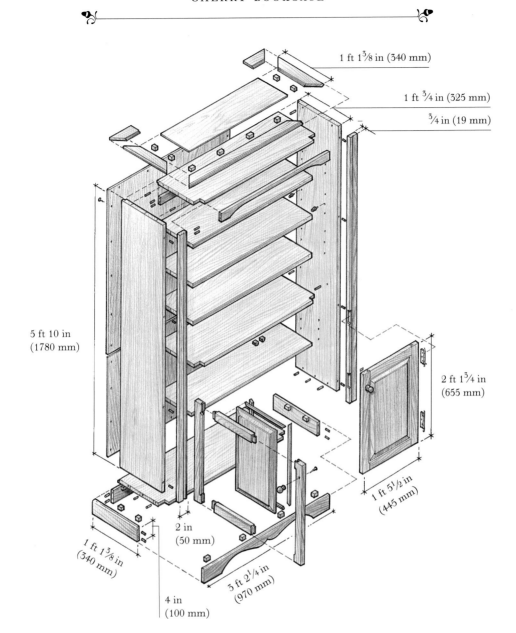

1 ft 1³⁄₈ in (340 mm)

1 ft ³⁄₄ in (325 mm)

³⁄₄ in (19 mm)

5 ft 10 in
(1780 mm)

2 ft 1³⁄₄ in
(655 mm)

1 ft 5¹⁄₂ in
(445 mm)

1 ft 1³⁄₈ in
(340 mm)

2 in
(50 mm)

4 in
(100 mm)

3 ft 2¹⁄₄ in
(970 mm)

Sanding and Finishing

In addition to using a belt sander and orbital sander, another useful tool for this project is a good scraper, as long as it is kept very sharp at all times. Working with cherry can present certain problems because its grain travels in two opposing directions, and the resulting "wooliness" often has to be scraped or sanded back to produce a smooth, even result. Cherry looks good with an oil finish. Apply two to three coats, allowing each to dry completely and sanding between coats with 400-grit sandpaper.

8 Glue and clamp up the stile and rail joints. Mark and cut door panels to 1 ft 7½ in (495 mm) length and plane them to fit the frame rabbets. Raise and field the panels to their front-facing edges all around, then position them in the rabbets. If you are staining the bookcase, stain the panels before fixing them, or shrinkage may show up unfinished edges. Cut ¼ in (6 mm) beading to fit around the join of the panels and frames, then fix in place using veneer nails. Fit 2 in (50 mm) brass finished flush hinges to the frames, and hang the doors from the upright fascias. Screw-fix pine handles to the door frames.

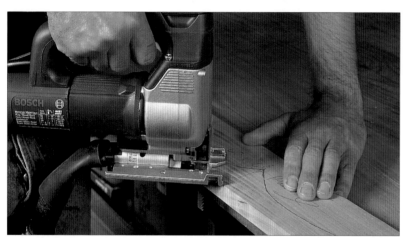

9 Mark and cut the plinth front and back to 3 ft 2¾ in (985 mm) and the sides to 1 ft 1⅜ in (340 mm) length. Make up a template as for the front top rail, and cut the plinth front to shape. Mark a line for the top of the glue blocks along the four parts, miter the corners of the four plinth parts to fit closely around the base of the carcass, apply glue and clamp up. Cut ten glue blocks to 1⅛ in (30 mm) length, and glue them along the inside edges of the plinth. Mark and cut the front and back of the cornice to 3 ft 2¾ in (985 mm) length, and sides to 1 ft 1⅜ in (340 mm).

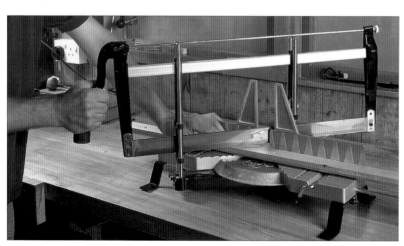

10 Miter the cornice corners to fit closely around the carcass base. Cut a rabbet along the top edge of the four parts, then mark a line for the glue blocks, apply glue and clamp up. Cut ten glue blocks and glue as for the plinth. Cut the dust board to 3 ft 2¼ in (970 mm), and screw it into place on the rabbet. Mark and cut ten bead and butt boards to 3 ft 9 in (1145 mm), glue together and fix to the top of the rabbeted area, using ¾ in (19 mm) no. 6 woodscrews. Cut the cupboard back plywood to 3 ft 2 in (965 mm), and screw in place. Fit the plinth and cornice.

LIST OF MATERIALS (*measurements indicate cut size*)

	SECTION	LENGTH
CABINET Cherry for top, cupboard top and bottom, 3	1 ft 1⅜ in x ¾ in (340 x 19 mm)	9 ft 5¾ in (2835 mm)
Cherry for sides, 2	1 ft ¾ in x ¾ in (325 x 19 mm)	11 ft 8 in (3560 mm)
Cherry for upper shelves, 3	1 ft ½ in x ¾ in (320 x 19 mm)	9 ft 5⅜ in (2829 mm)
Cherry for pot shelf, 1	11¼ x ¾ in (285 x 19 mm)	3 ft 1⅛ in (943 mm)
Cherry for front top rail, 1	4 x ¾ in (100 x 19 mm)	3 ft 1¼ in (945 mm)
Cherry for back top rail, 1, and upright fascias, 2	2 x ¾ in (50 x 19 mm)	14 ft 9¼ in (4505 mm)
Veneered bead and butt plywood for backs, 10	3¾ x ⅜ in (95 x 10 mm)	37 ft 6 in (11m 450 mm)
Plywood for cupboard back, 1	2 ft 1 in x ¼ in (635 x 6 mm)	3 ft 2 in (965 mm)
Cherry for plinth front and back, 2, and sides, 2	4 x ¾ in (100 x 19 mm)	8 ft 8¼ in (2650 mm)
Hardwood/softwood for glue blocks, 20	¾ x ¾ in (19 x 19 mm)	1 ft 10½ in (600 mm)
Fluted dowels	5/16 in (8 mm) in diameter	
Brass shelf inserts and lug supports, 12 No. 6 woodscrews	¾ in (19 mm)	
DOORS Cherry for stiles, 4, and rails, 4	2 x ¾ in (50 x 19 mm)	13 ft 7 in (4140 mm)
Cherry for panels, 2	1 ft 1¼ in x ¾ in (335 x 19 mm)	3 ft 3 in (990 mm)
Hardwood or softwood beading	¼ x ¼ in (6 x 6 mm)	11 ft 8 in (3560 mm)
Brass hinges with finials, 4 Pine wood handles, 2 Magnetic catches, 2	2 in (50 mm)	
CORNICE Cherry for front and back, 2, and sides, 2	2⅝ x ¾ in (67 x 19 mm)	8 ft 8¼ in (2650 mm)
Plywood for dustboard, 1	1 ft 1¼ in x ¼ in (335 x 6 mm)	3 ft 2¼ in (970 mm)

SIDE TABLE

This simple design uses mortise-and-tenon joints for the frame, and dovetail joints for the drawers. Consider using reclaimed wood for this project, as a weathered look fits well with the traditional design.

1 Cut the legs to 2 ft 9 in (840 mm) length. Cut two $\frac{5}{8}$-in (15-mm) wide mortises on each inside edge, the top mortises $\frac{5}{8}$ in (15 mm) from the top of the legs, and the lower ones $9\frac{3}{4}$ in (250 mm) from the top. Cut the four front and back rails to 3 ft $2\frac{3}{4}$ in (985 mm) and the four side rails to 1 ft $3\frac{1}{4}$ in (385 mm). Mark and cut tenons on the end of each rail, dry-assemble and check the frame.

2 Glue up the joints and clamp the frame. Next, cut the two drawer runners to 1 ft 5 in (430 mm) length. Apply glue to the bottom edge, and position and nail in place along the length of the lower side rails.

3 Cut the drawer guides to 1 ft $1\frac{3}{8}$ in (340 mm) length. Clamp the guides between the legs, next to the runners, then mark and drill three pilot holes from the bottom edge of the lower side rails. Remove the clamps, apply glue to the bottom edge of the guides, then clamp in place and add screws through the pilot holes.

4 Cut the eight glue blocks to $\frac{3}{4}$ in (19 mm) length, and glue them into place on the inside corners of the side rails and legs. The blocks on the lower side rails should fit snugly to the drawer guides, without projecting out past the legs and rails.

5 Cut the two side panels to 1 ft $2\frac{1}{2}$ in (370 mm) length, making sure that the corners are square. Hold the panels up to the sides to check their positions, then apply glue to the inside edges and nail in place.

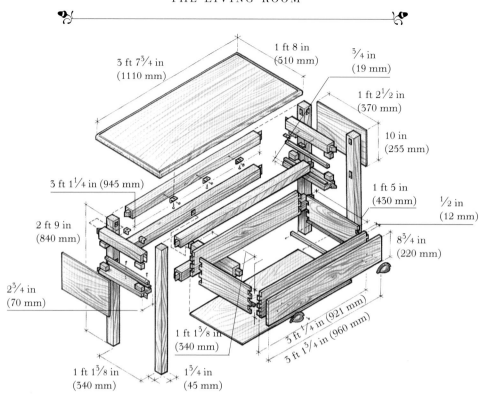

3 ft 7¾ in (1110 mm)

1 ft 8 in (510 mm)

¾ in (19 mm)

1 ft 2½ in (370 mm)

10 in (255 mm)

3 ft 1¼ in (945 mm)

1 ft 5 in (430 mm)

½ in (12 mm)

2 ft 9 in (840 mm)

8¾ in (220 mm)

2¾ in (70 mm)

1 ft 1⅜ in (340 mm)

3 ft ¼ in (921 mm)

3 ft 1¾ in (960 mm)

1 ft 1⅜ in (340 mm)

1¾ in (45 mm)

LIST OF MATERIALS (measurements indicate cut size)		
ITEM	**SECTION**	**LENGTH**
Hardwood/softwood for top, 1	1 ft 8 in x ¾ in (510 x 19 mm)	3 ft 7¾ in (1110 mm)
Softwood for top bearers, 3	1½ x ¾ in (38 x 19 mm)	3 ft 9 in (1140 mm)
Softwood for legs, 4	1¾ x 1¾ in (45 x 45 mm)	11 ft (3360 mm)
Softwood for front and back rails, 4, and side rails, 4	1¾ x 1 in (45 x 25 mm)	17 ft 6 in (5320 mm)
Softwood for drawer sides, 2, and front, 1	7½ x ½ in (190 x 12 mm)	5 ft 10¼ in (1701 mm)
Softwood for drawer back, 1	7⅛ x ½ in (180 x 12 mm)	3 ft ¼ in (921 mm)
Softwood for false drawer front, 1	8¾ x ⅜ in (220 x 10 mm)	3 ft 1¾ in (960 mm)
Plywood for drawer base, 1	1 ft 5 in x 3/16 in (430 x 4 mm)	3 ft ¼ in (921 mm)
Softwood for side panels, 2	9¾ x ¼ in (250 x 6 mm)	2 ft 5 in (740 mm)
Softwood for drawer guides, 2	1¾ x ¾ in (45 x 19 mm)	2 ft 2¾ in (680 mm)
Softwood for drawer runners, 2	⅜ x 3/16 in (10 x 4 mm)	2 ft 10 in (860 mm)
Softwood for blocks, 8	⅞ x ⅞ in (21 x 21 mm)	6 in (150 mm)
Angled brackets, 10, woodscrews, panel nails, brass handles, 2		

6 Cut the timber for the table top to 3 ft 7¾ in (1110 mm) length. Plane the surfaces flat, then glue and clamp together, using bar clamps. To prevent the top from bowing, cut three bearers to 1 ft 3 in (380 mm) length and glue and screw them to the underside of the top.

7 Cut a decorative molding along all four edges of the top, using a power router or by hand. The profile of the molding should not be too complicated for such a simple project; an ovolo cutter was used here, or you can use a roundover cutter.

8 Screw three angled steel brackets to the front and back top rails, to fit flush with the top surface, and two to the top side rails. Fit the top in position and drill pilot screw holes, then screw the top into place.

9 Cut the drawer front and back to 3 ft ¼ in (921 mm), and the drawer sides to 1 ft 5 in (430 mm) length. Cut dovetails in the ends, by hand or using a dovetail jig. Mark and cut a ³⁄₁₆ in (4 mm) groove ⅜ in (10 mm) from the bottom inside edge of the front and sides, then glue and clamp the drawer frame together, checking it for square.

10 Cut the false drawer front to 3 ft 1¾ in (960 mm), and cut a gentle round molding along all four edges. Apply glue and clamp it to the drawer front, then drill pilot holes and screw from the inside. Screw on the drawer pulls.

11 Cut the plywood drawer base to 3 ft ¼ in (921 mm). Apply glue to the front and side edges, then slide it into place in the groove on the drawer front and sides. Nail the back into place on the drawer back.

OAK COFFEE TABLE

This refectory-style coffee table can be made from hardwood or softwood, but oak looks very good. The top and magazine shelf are made from narrow panels of timber, and you can turn the legs or buy them preturned.

The magazine shelf rests on supports that are glued into the table legs.

1 Mark out and cut three 3 ft 6 in (1065 mm) lengths of 7 x 1 in (178 x 25 mm) timber for the top. Plane and number the boards for matching. Round the side boards at the corners. Mark the jointing edge of each board at 4–6 in (100–150 mm) intervals, then cut slots at each mark, using a biscuit joiner. Glue biscuits into the slots.

2 Apply glue to the edges and biscuits to be joined and clamp them up on the bench top, using two bar clamps at the ends of the upper surfaces and two more on the underside between them. Tighten all the clamps, checking that the boards are flat, and let dry, preferably overnight.

3 Release the clamps, check the top and plane the upper surface. Using a router, cut a decorative molding around the edge of the top. Mark out and cut two 2 ft 9 in (840 mm) lengths of 6 x ¾ in (150 x 19 mm) timber, and follow the procedures for assembling and routing the top. Measure out and cut two 3 ft 1 in (940 mm) lengths of timber for the side rails.

4 Mark out and cut two 1 ft 4 in (406 mm) lengths of timber for the end rails. Plane all the rails and mark out 1½ in (38 mm) from the ends of each of the rails, then cut a haunched tenon ¼ in (6 mm) wide. Cut the haunch from the top to ½ in (12 mm) deep and the same measurement long. Cut a decorative groove along the bottom of the outside face of each rail.

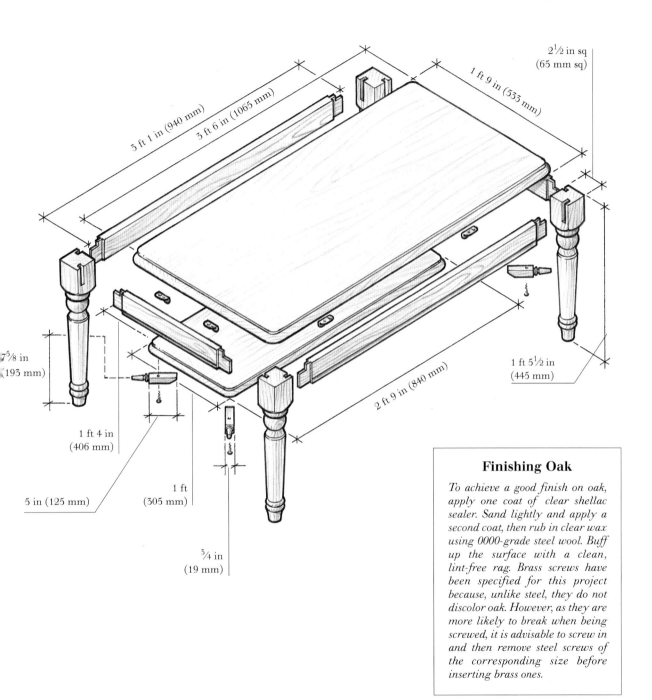

2½ in sq
(65 mm sq)

1 ft 9 in (533 mm)

3 ft 1 in (940 mm)

3 ft 6 in (1065 mm)

7⅝ in
(193 mm)

1 ft 5½ in
(445 mm)

2 ft 9 in (840 mm)

1 ft 4 in
(406 mm)

5 in (125 mm)

1 ft
(305 mm)

¾ in
(19 mm)

Finishing Oak

To achieve a good finish on oak, apply one coat of clear shellac sealer. Sand lightly and apply a second coat, then rub in clear wax using 0000-grade steel wool. Buff up the surface with a clean, lint-free rag. Brass screws have been specified for this project because, unlike steel, they do not discolor oak. However, as they are more likely to break when being screwed, it is advisable to screw in and then remove steel screws of the corresponding size before inserting brass ones.

5 You can either purchase 1 ft 5½-in (445-mm) long legs pre-turned or turn them yourself from 2½ x 2½ in (65 x 65 mm) timber on a lathe. In either case, you must make sure that the square section measures at least 2½ in (65 mm) from the top. Select the best surfaces to face out, then mark out for the haunched mortises on the other surfaces.

6 Drill and chop out the waste wood for the mortises using a ¼ in (6 mm) chisel, checking as you go, using the haunched tenons on each corresponding rail end. Mark and drill a ½-in (12-mm) diameter hole ¾ in (19 mm) deep on the inside diagonal of each leg, 7⅝ in (193 mm) from the bottom.

7 Dry-assemble the legs and rails, using bar clamps with a piece of scrap wood inside each clamp face. With the joints pulled up, check that no gaps show and that all the components are straight, using a setsquare. Make any adjustments, disassemble the frame, apply glue, clamp up again and let dry.

8 Mark out and cut four 6½ in (165 mm) lengths for the shelf supports. Round between ¾ and 1½ in (19 and 38 mm) from one end of each piece, and check that the ¾ in (19 mm) end fits into the drilled leg hole. Mark and cut a decorative acute-angled miter on the other end if required. Drill a central screw hole 2 in (50 mm) from this end, apply glue to the leg hole and fit the support.

9 Drill screw holes and fix stretcher plates to the top of the inside side and end rails. Position the shelf on the supports and mark through the screw holes. Remove the shelf, drill screw holes, then glue and screw shelf to supports. Place the top in position and mark through stretcher plates for screws on the underside. Remove the top, drill the screw holes and screw the top to the frame.

LIST OF MATERIALS (*measurements indicate cut size*)		
ITEM	SECTION	LENGTH
Hardwood/softwood for top, 1	1 ft 9 in x 1 in (534 x 25 mm)	3 ft 6 in (1065 mm)
Hardwood/softwood for shelf, 1	1 ft x ¾ in (305 x 19 mm)	2 ft 9 in (840 mm)
Hardwood/softwood for legs, 4	2½ x 2½ in (65 x 65 mm)	5 ft 10 in (1780 mm)
Hardwood/softwood for side rails, 2, and end rails, 2	2¼ x ¾ in (55 x 19 mm)	8 ft 10 in (2692 mm)
Hardwood/softwood for shelf supports, 4	¾ x ¾ in (19 x 19 mm)	2 ft 2 in (660 mm)
Biscuits		
Brass stretcher plates, 8, with brass screws No. 8 brass screws	½ in (12 mm) 1¼ in (32 mm)	

DOUBLE DISPLAY SHELF

*This simple but attractive shelf can be constructed in quite a short time,
using basic hand tools and softwood joined by hardwood dowels. You can
adapt both the curves of the ends and the dimensions as required.*

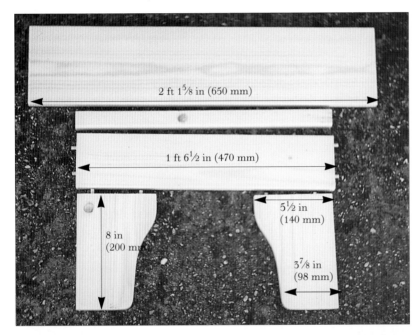

2 ft 1⅝ in (650 mm)

1 ft 6½ in (470 mm)

5½ in (140 mm)

8 in (200 mm)

3⅞ in (98 mm)

1 First, draw a ⅜ x ⅜ in (10 x 10 mm) grid on a piece of cardboard and mark out the curves of the side pieces. Cut out the template, transfer it to the 5½ x ¾ in (140 x 19 mm) timber and cut two 8 in (200 mm) lengths. Cut out the curves as close to the drawn line as possible, using a coping saw.

2 Mark and cut the top shelf to 2 ft 1⅝ in (650 mm) length from 5¾ x ¾ in (145 x 19 mm) timber, the bottom shelf to 1 ft 6½ in (470 mm) length from 3¾ x ¾ in (95 x 19 mm) timber, and the hanging rail to 1 ft 6½ in (470 mm) length from 1⅝ x ¾ in (40 x 19 mm) timber. Plane a square finish on the two shelves, or round, or chamfer them.

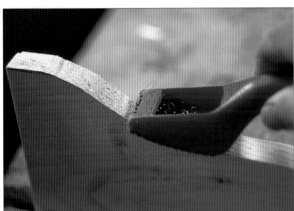

3 Next, smooth the curves on the shelves by using a shaping tool, or a rasp, or a file. To finish off, wrap some sandpaper around a sanding block or a short length of round pole, and sand.

4 On the top edges of the sides, mark out dowel hole centers 1⅛ in (30 mm) from the front and back. Bore out ¼-in (6-mm) diameter holes ½ in (12 mm) deep, using a depth stop or marker on the bit. Use a try square to ensure that the hole is bored vertically.

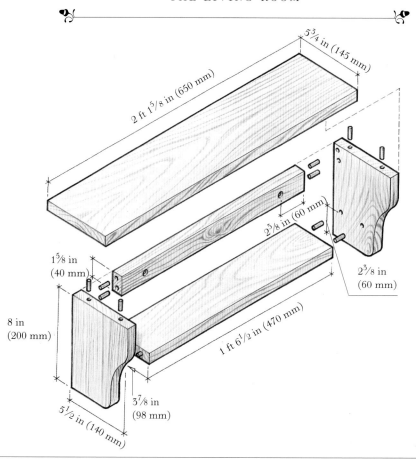

5³⁄₄ in (145 mm)

2 ft 1⁵⁄₈ in (650 mm)

2³⁄₈ in (60 mm)

2³⁄₈ in (60 mm)

1⁵⁄₈ in (40 mm)

8 in (200 mm)

1 ft 6¹⁄₂ in (470 mm)

5¹⁄₂ in (140 mm)

3⁷⁄₈ in (98 mm)

An Authentic Finish

After sanding the finished shelf with fine sandpaper, you can apply clear or colored varnish, stain, or colored polish, or paint it. If using colored varnish or stain, first test the finish on a piece of scrap wood the same as that used for the project – perhaps the offcuts from the sides.

To fix the finished display shelf to a wall, mark out two holes in the hanging rail, 2 ³⁄₈ in (60 mm) in from the sides and ³⁄₄ in (19 mm) from the bottom of the top shelf. Drill through the hanging rail, then use screws and wall plugs to hang the shelf.

LIST OF MATERIALS *(measurements indicate cut size)*		
ITEM	**SECTION**	**LENGTH**
Softwood for top shelf, 1	5³⁄₄ x ³⁄₄ in (145 x 19 mm)	2 ft 1⁵⁄₈ in (650 mm)
Softwood for bottom shelf, 1	3³⁄₄ x ³⁄₄ in (95 x 19 mm)	1 ft 6¹⁄₂ in (470 mm)
Softwood for hanging rail, 1	1⁵⁄₈ x ³⁄₄ in (40 x 19 mm)	1 ft 6¹⁄₂ in (470 mm)
Softwood for sides, 2	5¹⁄₂ x ³⁄₄ in (140 x 19 mm)	1 ft 4 in (400 mm)
Hardwood dowels, 12	¼ in (6 mm) diameter	
Dowel nails	¼ in (6 mm) diameter	

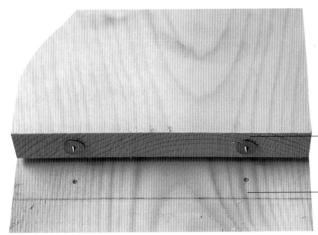

Dowel nails
pressed into
dowel holes

First guideline
across shelf
bottom

5 Use ¼ in (6 mm) diameter dowel nails to mark the corresponding holes in the bottom of the top shelf. Press the nails into the dowel holes in the sides. Mark two lines across the bottom shelf, 3½ in (90 mm) in from the ends, then two more lines ¾ in (19 mm) further in. Fit the top shelf edges inside the lines, and push them in to make dowel marks.

6 Mark in pencil and bore out the ¼ in (6 mm) mating holes in the top shelf again using a try square to ensure that the drill bit is kept on a vertical plane. Fit the dowels into the sides and check that they match the holes in the shelf accurately.

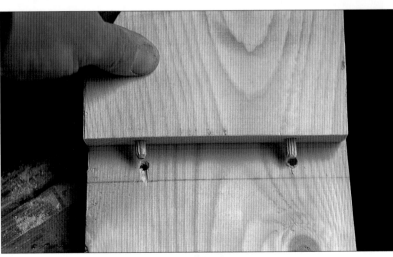

7 Mark and drill two dowel holes in the ends of the hanging rail, with the centers ⅜ in (10 mm) from the top and bottom, and two holes in the ends of the bottom shelf, with their centers ¾ in (19 mm) from each end. Drill the dowel holes and fit dowel nails, then match to the sides and drill mating holes. Apply adhesive to all the parts and clamp them together, checking for square.

MANTELPIECE

An elegant mantelpiece creates a focus in a living room, whether used it houses a fire or is purely ornamental. The measurements given here are intended as a guide to proportions – you can adapt them to suit your individual requirements.

1 Mark out and cut to length the two pillar fronts from 5¾ x ¾ in (145 x 19 mm) timber and the four sides from 1¾ x ¾ in (45 x 19 mm). These pillars run right up through to the underside of the mantel board. If the sides require any further cutting, to overlap or fit existing wall or floor fittings, mark and cut them at this stage.

2 Cut four cleats for each pillar, either ripping down 1¾ x ¾ in (45 x 19 mm) offcuts or using 1⅜ x ¾ in (35 x 19 mm) timber. The cleats must be a tight fit inside the sides. Cut some waste wood to the same length as the cleats, to give extra support for decorative moldings on the pillar fronts. Drill pilot holes through the fronts to mark where this extra support will go.

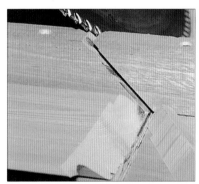

3 Start the boxes by marking a line ⅜ in (10 mm) out from the edge down the back face edge of the front boards. Drill four countersunk clearance holes each side through to the face. The holes at the bottom of the pillar will be hidden by the skirting. Glue and clamp up the front and one side, then insert and tighten up the screws. Repeat for the other side.

4 Fit the cleats and supports, using plenty of glue and knocking them into place with a hammer. Nail them if they are loose, working from the outside in, then sink the nail heads and fill the holes.

5 Cut to length and miter-cut the reversible skirting. Cutting miters can be tricky using only a miter box, so use a sliding miter saw, or a motorized cross-cut saw with the blade set at 45°. The two returns can be cut a bit longer than the sides.

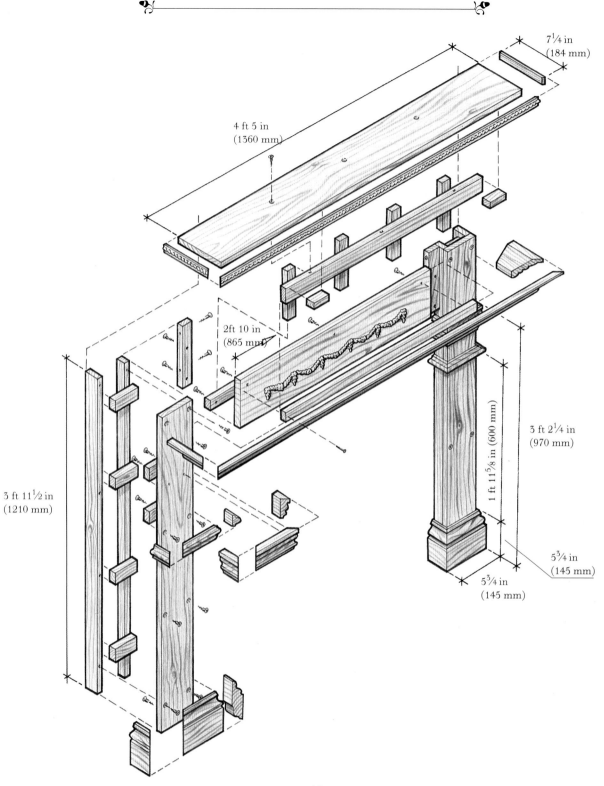

7¼ in
(184 mm)

4 ft 5 in
(1360 mm)

2ft 10 in
(865 mm)

3 ft 2¼ in
(970 mm)

1 ft 11⅝ in (600 mm)

3 ft 11½ in
(1210 mm)

5¾ in
(145 mm)

5¾ in
(145 mm)

6 Sand off excess glue and filler before fitting any moldings. Fit the skirting, front piece first, using plenty of glue and a couple of screws driven in from the back. Nail on the side pieces, and again add one screw from the back if required. Finish off by sinking any nail heads and filling all holes.

7 Following the same routine, cut and fit the architrave and small decorative molding. Nails should hold the architrave, but put a screw in from the back if necessary. When the glue has hardened, trim off the pieces of the moldings that extend past the back edge of the pillars. Clean off any excess filler or glue and smooth rough edges.

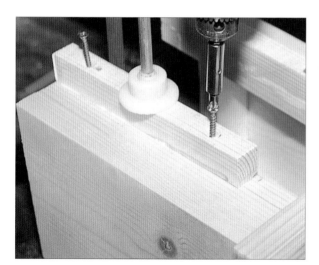

8 Cut and fit one piece of $1\frac{3}{4}$ x $\frac{3}{4}$ in (45 x 19 mm) to the inside edge of each pillar, flush with the top and back, using screws and glue. Cut the center board to the length required between the pillars from $7\frac{1}{4}$ x $\frac{3}{4}$ in (184 x 19 mm) timber and the support from $1\frac{3}{8}$ x $\frac{3}{4}$ in (35 x 19 mm) timber. Cut two additional pieces out of the smaller section.

9 Fix one of the smaller pieces with screws and glue to the back bottom edge of the center board. Turn the pillars face down. At the bottom join them at the exact width, using a piece of waste as a spacer. This will provide support for the pillars.

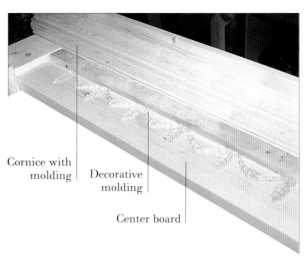

Cornice with molding | Decorative molding | Center board

10 At the top fix the center board from the back with screws and glue, making sure that all is square before finally fixing. Fix the other $1\frac{3}{8}$ x $\frac{3}{4}$ in (35 x 19 mm) length to the face of the center board, $2\frac{3}{4}$ in (70 mm) down from the top. Depending upon actual sizes, this piece may need to be reduced or increased in thickness; it must finish flush with the front surface of the pillars so that the cornice will fit tight against it.

11 Cut and fix a couple of glue blocks on each side into the gap at the top above the center board. Cut another piece of $1\frac{3}{8}$ x $\frac{3}{4}$ in (35 x 19 mm) timber to length and fix this to the blocks. Mark and cut the mantel board to size from $7\frac{1}{4}$ x $\frac{3}{4}$ in (184 x 19 mm) timber, and decide which face will be the top. If there is any cupping in the board, it is better to have this facing up so that objects run toward the center rather than off the sides.

12 Mark a line on the underside of the mantel to corres-pond with the center of the bearer fixed to the top of the pillars. Drill and countersink three fixing holes, and glue and screw the board into place. For extra support, cut some blocks and affix with glue by simply rubbing them into place, but don't make them too large to obstruct the cornice. Fit the decorations on the center board into place by gluing and rubbing them. Fill any screw and nail holes.

13 Mark and make a couple of trial cuts in the cornice pieces until you get the angles right. When happy with the fit, nail and glue them into place, then glue and screw the cornice into place. Cut and fit the dentil mold-ing to cover the heads of any screws that show.

14 Cut, then glue and nail the decorative molding around the front and side edges of the mantel board, pre-drilling the nail holes to avoid splitting the molding. Clean up the whole mantelpiece and finish.

LIST OF MATERIALS (*measurements indicate cut size. No lengths are given, as each mantelpiece will have varying dimensions.*)

ITEM	SECTION
Softwood for pillar fronts, 2	$5\frac{3}{4}$ in x $\frac{3}{4}$ in (145 x 19 mm)
Softwood for pillar sides, 4, and center board supports, 2	$1\frac{3}{4}$ x $\frac{3}{4}$ in (45 x 19 mm)
Softwood for mantel, 1, and center board, 1	$7\frac{1}{4}$ x $\frac{3}{4}$ in (184 x 19 mm)
Softwood for cleats, 8, center board bearers, 2, and glue blocks	$1\frac{3}{8}$ x $\frac{3}{4}$ in (35 x 19 mm)
Molded softwood for reversible skirting	$5\frac{3}{4}$ x $\frac{7}{8}$ in (145 x 21 mm)
Molded softwood bullnose architrave for cornice	$1\frac{3}{4}$ x $\frac{5}{8}$ in (45 x 15 mm)
Dentil molding for cornice	
Decorative molding for center board	
Decorative molding for pillars	
Woodscrews	
Fine wood nails	

Finishing

Treat anything that looks vaguely like a knot or is slightly resinous, using wood sealer. Let dry, then coat the mantelpiece with primer. When dry, lightly sand and coat with a white basecoat, lightly sanding again when dry. Additional coats should be applied when the mantelpiece has been fixed in place.

INLAID TABLE

The construction of this elegant coffee table is relatively simple. The marquetry and veneering are in the Sheraton style of the late eighteenth century, and use cross- and edge-banding, stringing, and a central fan motif.

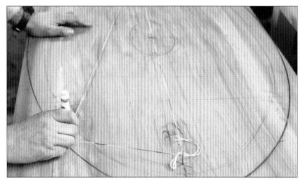

1 Mark and cut the boards for the top overlong and overwide, and plane the edges perfectly square and straight. Apply glue to the edges and clamp up, using bar clamps both above and below, to prevent cupping. Take particular care that the top is flat at all stages.

2 When the top is dry, draw the oval shape on it. This is best achieved by using two nails and string, adjusting the distance between the nails to get the required shape of oval, which is 4 ft x 2 ft 2 in (1220 x 660 mm).

3 Again using the nails and string, mark out the positions for the cross- and edge-banding and the central motif. Cut out the oval shape of the table top using a bandsaw as shown, and clean it up by hand with a plane and a rasp or a shaping tool. Use the top to mark out and cut two plywood templates, one for the middle rails and the other for the end rails.

4 Cut the middle rails to 2 ft $11\frac{3}{8}$ in (900 mm) and end rails to 1 ft $11\frac{5}{8}$ in (600 mm). Drill dowel holes in the meeting ends of end rails, then cut tenons in the other ends. Insert dowels and glue up the end rails. Cut tenons at both ends of the middle rails. Cut a $\frac{3}{8}$ in (10 mm) groove the same distance from the top of all rails.

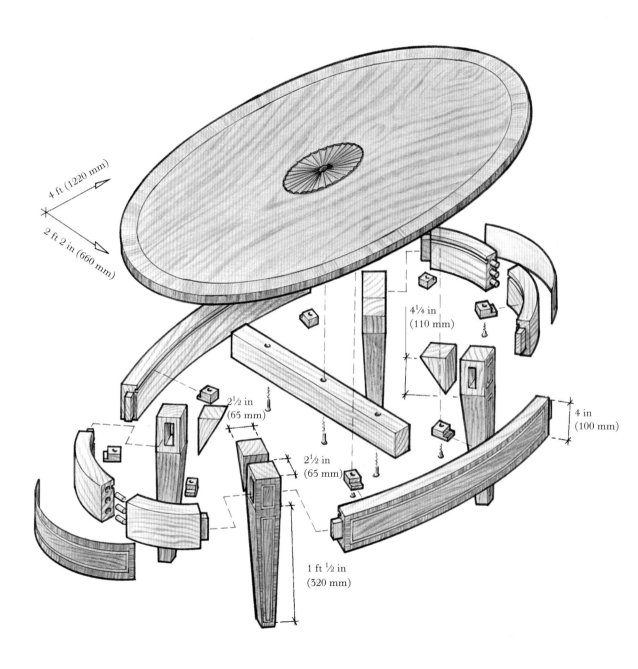

4 ft (1220 mm)

2 ft 2 in (660 mm)

4¼ in (110 mm)

2½ in (65 mm)

2½ in (65 mm)

4 in (100 mm)

1 ft ½ in (320 mm)

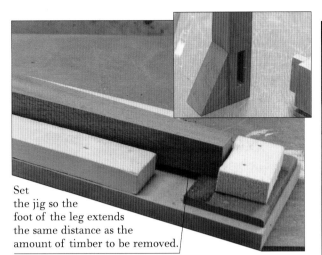

Set the jig so the foot of the leg extends the same distance as the amount of timber to be removed.

5 Cut legs to 1 ft 4⅝ in (420 mm) length. Cut the taper on inner edge and sides, leaving the outside face straight and the top of each leg square. If using a thicknesser, make a jig as shown above. Mark and cut mortises for middle and end rails in the sides of each leg. For extra leg support, cut four leg shoulders to 4¼ in (110 mm) length and to wedge shapes (see inset). Cut center rail to 1 ft (305 mm) length, and drill a screw hole at each end.

6 Dry-assemble the rails and legs, making any final adjustments, then glue and clamp up the frame. Mark and cut out a ⅝ x ⅜ in (15 x 10 mm) rabbet in the timber for the wood buttons, and then cut eight 1⅝ in (40 mm) lengths. Drill screw holes through the buttons.

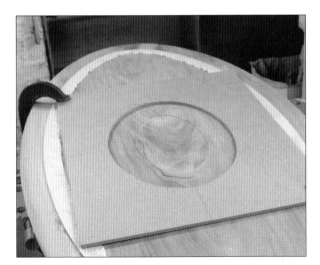

7 The veneer for the top is inlaid. Fit a wide cutter into a router to cut a very shallow rabbet to the exact depth of the cross-band veneer. Make two jigs for the central oval motif: one to router the shape into the top, and the other as a template for the marquetry motif itself. When cutting the oval shape, work very delicately, because the surface must be completely clean.

8 Lay the edge-banding first and then the cross-banding, using animal glue and a veneer hammer. Tape in place and allow to dry overnight, and then use a ³⁄₃₂ in (1.8 mm) cutter to cut grooves for the stringing in the top. Glue in the stringing. For the legs and frame, prepare the cross-banding and stringing first, then apply glue and fit the veneer onto the surfaces.

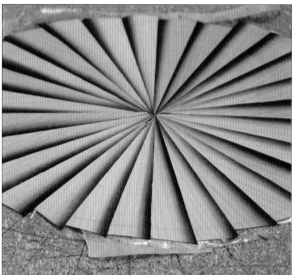

10 For the fan, draw out a full-size template on a board and use this to cut oversized wedge-shaped segments. To achieve an even gradient of shading through the veneer, allowing it to be sanded when in place, heat up fine sand in a cast iron pan, and carefully dip each segment into this, thus singeing the edge.

11 Build up the fan by cutting each segment and securing it in position with adhesive tape. Use the template to mark the oval shape of the fan, and a coin as a template to cut out the oval rosewood veneer center and the semicircular rosewood ends to the fan segments. Tape these in position and check very carefully for accuracy.

12 Cut the stringing for the fan to length, apply PVA glue to the fan and stringing, and hold it in position with weights. When everything is dry, lightly sand the whole table top, ready for assembly to the frame.

13 Position the frame on the underside of the top, then screw through the center rail. Fit the wood buttons into the groove in the middle and end rails, and screw them to the top; this traditional method allows for timber movement in the top without it splitting. You can also shape end blocks and glue them to the end-rail joints.

LIST OF MATERIALS (*measurements indicate cut size*)

TABLE	SECTION	LENGTH
Figured mahogany for top, 1	2 ft 2 in x $^3/_4$ in (660 x 19 mm)	4 ft (1220 mm)
Hardwood for legs, 4	$2^1/_2$ x $2^1/_2$ in (65 x 65 mm)	5 ft $6^1/_2$ in (1680 mm)
Hardwood for middle rails, 2, and end rails, 4	4 x $3^1/_8$ in (100 x 80 mm)	13 ft $9^1/_4$ in (4200 mm)
Hardwood for center rail, 1	$3^1/_8$ x $1^5/_8$ in (80 x 40 mm)	1 ft (305 mm)
Hardwood for wood buttons, 8	$1^5/_8$ x $^3/_4$ in (40 x 19 mm)	1 ft 1 in (320 mm)
Hardwood for leg shoulder wedges, 4	$2^1/_2$ x $2^1/_2$ in (65 x 65 mm)	1 ft 5 in (440 mm)
Doweling		
Woodscrews		
VENEERS		
Mahogany for frame and legs, 2	$11^3/_4$ in (300 mm) wide	6 ft $6^3/_4$ in (2000 mm)
Sycamore/harewood for oval cross-band, 1	$11^3/_4$ in (300 mm) wide	3 ft $3^5/_8$ in (997 mm)
Rosewood for oval edge-band, 1	8 in (200 mm) wide	$11^3/_4$ in (300 mm)
Black and white herringbone for stringing, 10	$^5/_{32}$ x $^5/_{32}$ in (1.8 x 1.8 mm)	32 ft $9^3/_4$ in (10 m)

Creating an Antique Finish

An antique finish is an important element in establishing the period and style of a finished piece of furniture, and in particular will maximize the effect of the marquetry. The method employed in this project used the traditional materials of French polish and linseed oil. These give a beautiful, rich glow to any piece of furniture, and emphasize the natural grain and color of the wood.

However, be warned that achieving a satisfactory French-polish finish is notoriously difficult for the beginner – in addition to ensuring that each application is smooth and even, the working area must be kept completely dust-

free, otherwise the finish will spoil as it hardens. However, the result certainly complements the veneers. As French polishing is a specialist discipline, bear in mind that the instructions here are intended as a brief outline only.

First, gently distress the surface. Apply linseed oil to the whole table followed by an oil-based stain. Carefully wipe this off using denatured alcohol, which creates shaded areas that give the impression of age. Finally, apply three or more coats of French polish, using button and garnet polishes to achieve the required degree of antique patina, and sanding between each coat.

DRAWER BENCH

This versatile storage seat was originally designed to fit beneath a window, but it can be used wherever it is needed. The construction includes mitered tenons and grooves for the carcass, and dovetail joints for the single drawer.

1 Cut the legs to 1 ft 4 in (406 mm) length, then clamp together in pairs or all four, as preferred. Mark out for two 1⅞-in (47-mm) wide mortises on the inside faces of each leg: the top mortises should start ¼ in (6 mm) from the top edge, and the lower ones should start 11¾ in (300 mm) from the top.

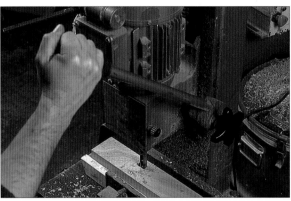

2 Cut the mortises, either by hand or using a mortising machine, and clean up with a sharp chisel. Mark out a central ⅜-in (10-mm) wide groove between each top and bottom mortise, and cut the grooves ⅜ in (10 mm) deep; a router makes this job quick and easy.

3 Cut the two front and two back rails to 2 ft 8 ¾ in (830 mm), and the four side rails to 1 ft 6 in (460 mm). Cut a 1⅞ in (47 mm) mitered tenon at each end of all the rails. Dry-assemble the frame and mark the top edge of each rail, then disassemble. Mark and cut a ⅜ in (10 mm) groove on the inside of each top rail, ⅜ in (10 mm) below the top, for the fixing buttons.

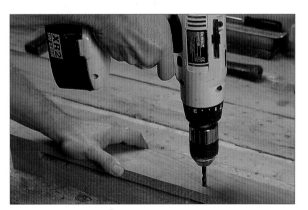

4 On the back and side rails, mark and cut a central ⅜ in (10 mm) groove along the bottom edge of the top rails and the top of the bottom rails, for the panels. Next, dry-assemble the frame again, and mark and then drill ¼ in (6 mm) diameter drawbore holes through the mortises in the legs and the tenons in the rails. Cut 16 dowels of the same diameter to length.

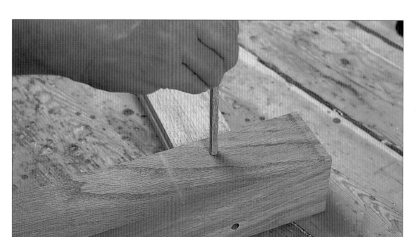

5 Glue and clamp the front legs and bottom rail together, using bar clamps and checking for square, then apply glue to the dowels and fit them into place. Repeat the process for the back legs and bottom rail, and let dry.

6 Mark and cut the back panel to 2 ft $7\frac{1}{2}$ in (805 mm) length and the side panels to 1 ft 3 in (380 mm) length. Field each side of the panels, finishing off with a $\frac{3}{8}$ in (10 mm) edge to fit the grooves in the legs and rails.

7 Glue up the panel edges and remaining tenons, and assemble and clamp the frame, applying glue to the dowels and inserting them as before. Check the frame for square and adjust as necessary, then let dry.

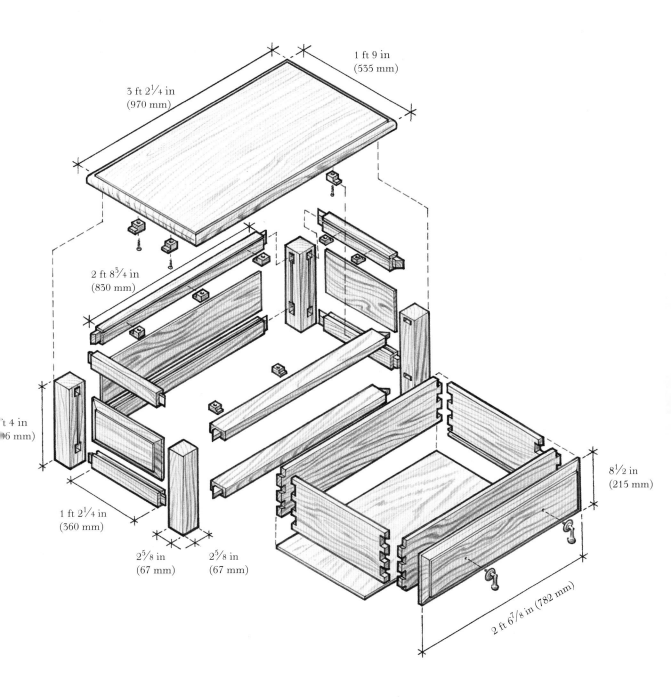

1 ft 9 in
(535 mm)

3 ft 2¼ in
(970 mm)

2 ft 8¾ in
(830 mm)

t 4 in
6 mm)

1 ft 2¼ in
(360 mm)

2⅝ in
(67 mm)

2⅝ in
(67 mm)

8½ in
(215 mm)

2 ft 6⅞ in (782 mm)

8 Cut the wood for the top to 3 ft 2$\frac{1}{4}$ in (970 mm) length. Cut a decorative molding around the entire edge – here, a roundover cutter was used. Cut 10 buttons as shown, with a $\frac{3}{8}$ in (10 mm) 'lip' for fitting into the top rail grooves. Lay the top onto the frame and position and glue three buttons along the front and back, and two along the sides. Mark through the screw holes in the buttons, then drill guide holes and screw the top onto the frame through the button holes.

9 Next, mark and cut the drawer sides to 1 ft 4 in (406 mm) and the front and back to 2 ft 6$\frac{3}{4}$ in (780 mm). Cut dovetails at each end, by hand or using a dovetail jig and router.

10 Mark and cut a $\frac{3}{16}$ in (4 mm) groove $\frac{3}{4}$ in (19 mm) from the bottom edge of the front and sides, to take the plywood base. Apply glue to the dovetails, then clamp up and assemble the drawer frame. When dry, cut the base to size, slide it into position from the back, and tack it to the bottom edge of the back.

11 Mark and cut the false drawer front to size, and cut a decorative molding around all four sides. Glue and clamp it to the drawer front, then drill pilot holes from the inside and reinforce with woodscrews. Mark and drill holes in the false front for two brass handles, and screw these in place.

LIST OF MATERIALS (*measurements indicate cut size*)

ITEM	SECTION	LENGTH
Hardwood/softwood for top, 1	1 ft 9 in x $^{7}/_{8}$ in (535 x 21 mm)	3 ft 2$^{1}/_{4}$ in (970 mm)
Hardwood/softwood for legs, 4	2$^{5}/_{8}$ x 2$^{5}/_{8}$ in (67 x 67 mm)	5 ft 4 in (1624 mm)
Hardwood/softwood for front rails, 2, and back rails, 2	2 $^{3}/_{8}$ x 1$^{1}/_{8}$ in (60 x 30 mm)	10 ft 11 in (3320 mm)
Hardwood/softwood for side rails, 4	2$^{3}/_{8}$ x 1$^{1}/_{8}$ in (60 x 30 mm)	6 ft (1840 mm)
Hardwood/softwood for drawer sides and front, 3	7 x $^{1}/_{2}$ in (178 x 12 mm)	5 ft 2$^{3}/_{4}$ in (1596 mm)
Hardwood/softwood for drawer back, 1	6$^{3}/_{4}$ x $^{1}/_{2}$ in (170 x 12 mm)	2 ft 6$^{3}/_{4}$ in (780 mm)
Hardwood/softwood for false drawer front, 1	8$^{1}/_{2}$ x 1 in (215 x 25 mm)	2 ft 8$^{1}/_{4}$ in (820 mm)
Plywood for drawer base, 1	1 ft 4 in x $^{3}/_{16}$ in (406 x 4 mm)	2 ft 6$^{3}/_{4}$ in (780 mm)
Hardwood/softwood for side and back panels, 3	9$^{1}/_{2}$ x $^{3}/_{4}$ in (240 x 19 mm)	5 ft 1$^{1}/_{2}$ in (1565 mm)
Hardwood/softwood for buttons, 10	1 x $^{3}/_{4}$ in (25 x 19 mm)	10 in (255 mm)
Doweling	$^{1}/_{4}$ in (6 mm) diameter	
Brass handles, 2		
Woodscrews		

Finishing

This project looks particularly good with a simple clear wax finish. To achieve this, apply knot sealer if required, then two coats of sanding sealer, sanding with very fine sandpaper after each coat, then rub in the wax. For a more hard-wearing finish, use wood varnish, possibly after applying a suitable woodstain.

WINDSOR ARMCHAIR

These chairs were traditionally made from a variety of native woods, with elm, beech, yew, and ash often being used in the same chair. The construction involves turning and steam-bending, and the result is a classic design.

The long sticks pass through the armrest bow.

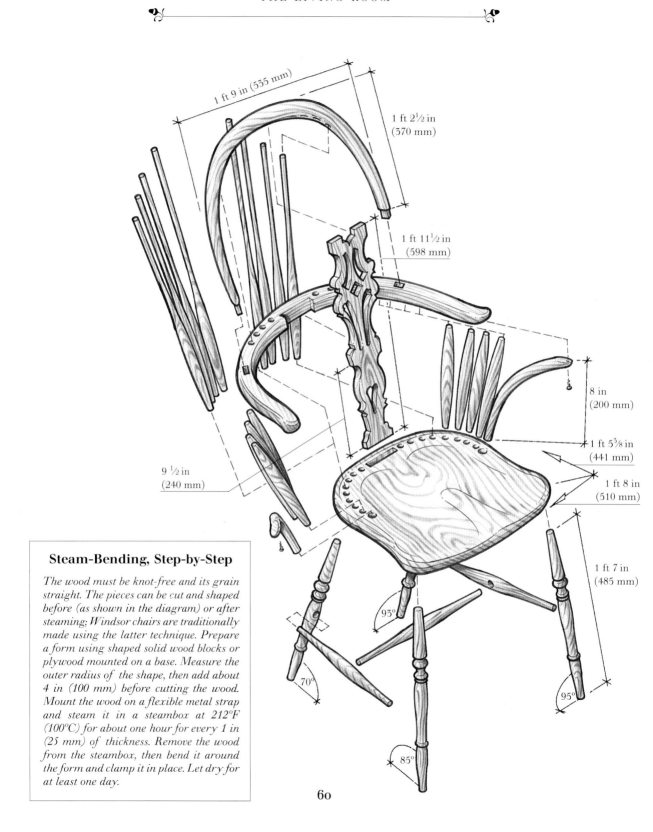

1 ft 9 in (535 mm)

1 ft 2½ in (370 mm)

1 ft 11½ in (598 mm)

8 in (200 mm)

1 ft 5⅜ in (441 mm)

1 ft 8 in (510 mm)

9 ½ in (240 mm)

1 ft 7 in (485 mm)

93°

70°

95°

85°

Steam-Bending, Step-by-Step

The wood must be knot-free and its grain straight. The pieces can be cut and shaped before (as shown in the diagram) or after steaming; Windsor chairs are traditionally made using the latter technique. Prepare a form using shaped solid wood blocks or plywood mounted on a base. Measure the outer radius of the shape, then add about 4 in (100 mm) before cutting the wood. Mount the wood on a flexible metal strap and steam it in a steambox at 212°F (100°C) for about one hour for every 1 in (25 mm) of thickness. Remove the wood from the steambox, then bend it around the form and clamp it in place. Let dry for at least one day.

60

1 Cut and shape the seat, varying the width between $1\frac{1}{2}$ in (38 mm) at the edges and $\frac{1}{2}$ in (12 mm). Cut the legs to 1 ft 7 in (485 mm), then turn each blank on a lathe before building up the features using gouges and skew chisels. Trim down the tops of the legs to 1 in (25 mm) diameter, using a rounding-off tool. Cut the side stretchers to 1 ft $2\frac{7}{8}$ in (377 mm) and the center stretcher to 1 ft $4\frac{3}{8}$ in (415 mm), and turn them to shape.

2 Hold the seat in the vice with the bottom facing out, and level the marks for the holes for the back pair of legs to the line of the bench top. Clamp a sheet of plywood to a trestle and align its top edge exactly with the centers of the holes and the bench top. Take the angles of splay from the illustration and mark the offsets to the side, using an angle bevel. Drill the holes to 1 in (25 mm) diameter, but do not drill through the seat. Fit the legs to the seat, then establish the position for the side stretchers.

3 Mark the sides of the legs with the angles of the side stretcher hole; sight down the legs from above to mark the center point. Drill the holes, trim the stretchers to length and push them into place: insert the front leg, insert the stretcher, then press the back leg into position, locating the stretcher. Mark the position and angles for the center stretcher, drill the holes in the side stretchers, and fit the center stretcher. Mark and number each part. Mark a depth line on each leg, apply glue, and assemble.

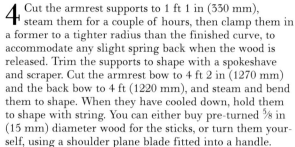

4 Cut the armrest supports to 1 ft 1 in (330 mm), steam them for a couple of hours, then clamp them in a former to a tighter radius than the finished curve, to accommodate any slight spring back when the wood is released. Trim the supports to shape with a spokeshave and scraper. Cut the armrest bow to 4 ft 2 in (1270 mm) and the back bow to 4 ft (1220 mm), and steam and bend them to shape. When they have cooled down, hold them to shape with string. You can either buy pre-turned $\frac{5}{8}$ in (15 mm) diameter wood for the sticks, or turn them yourself, using a shoulder plane blade fitted into a handle.

5 Cut the sticks slightly overlength: the eight long ones to 1 ft 11$\frac{1}{2}$ in (598 mm), and the eight short ones to 1 ft (305 mm). To fit the armrest bow, mark off and drill the holes for the armrest supports, using angle bevels to find the right line. Trim them until they slide tightly into the holes. Drill a $\frac{1}{8}$ in (4 mm) hole into the side of the seat and through the supports, and insert a long nail that can easily be withdrawn to hold them in place. Mark and trim the supports flat on their upper surfaces. Make a temporary support to hold the back arc of the armrest bow with its height relative to the seat, its angle, and its center line. Drill and screw the bow to the supports from underneath.

6 Mark and drill the holes for the short sticks in the armrest bow to $\frac{1}{2}$ in (12 mm) depth, and chop out the slot in the seat to house the back splat. Cut the splat to 1 ft 11$\frac{1}{2}$ in (598 mm), and shape the top and bottom to fit into the seat and back bow; cut out and shape the splat decorations using a fretsaw. Tap the splat, which is tapered downward, into the seat slot and mark off the recess in the armrest to hold it. Use a temporary former beneath the armrest bow, to hold it steady. Cut the slot in the armrest carefully, and ease the splat into position.

7 Mark and drill the holes for the sticks in the seat, about $\frac{1}{2}$ in (12 mm) deep. Mark the positions of the long sticks on the armrest, and drill the holes through, making sure that they are set well back. Replace the arm rest and sight through the holes for the positions of the long sticks. Taper the short sticks a little, trim to length, and fit them into the seat and armrest. Number each stick and mark its orientation against the seat. Remove the arm rest and fit the long sticks; lower the armrest onto the support and fit the short sticks.

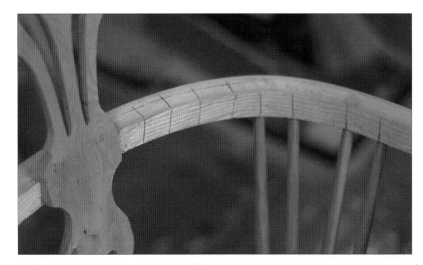

8 Remove the long sticks, refasten the armrest, and insert the back splat. Mark the height of the back bow on the top edge of the splat. Remove the string tying the ends of the bow, hold it in position and mark off on its ends the angle at which they meet the armrest. Trim these angles and use a spokeshave or draw knife to shape the inner curves of the bow, tapering it toward its ends. At the inside edges of the ends, shape the bow so that it appears to conform to the inward curve of the armrest. Mark the tenon shoulders 2 ft (610 mm) from the center of the bow, and then mark the positions and center lines of the mortises on the armrest, which should be $\frac{3}{8}$ in (10 mm) wide.

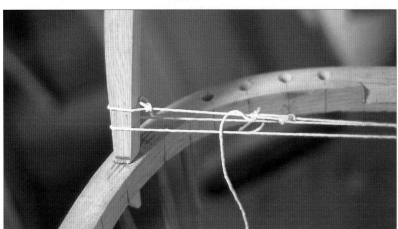

9 Place the bow in position, mark the angles of the mortises on its ends, then shade and cut the tenon cheeks, stopping about $\frac{1}{4}$ in (6 mm) short of the shoulder lines. Remove the waste and square up the ends of the tenons. Place the bow in position and, with the tenons centered over the mortise marks, trace around the tenons to give the exact mortise shape. With the arm rest in place, drill and chop out the mortises using a $\frac{1}{4}$ in (6 mm) chisel, and trim the tenons to fit.

10 Lower the bow gently into place, adjusting for fit. With the bow touching the top of the splat, mark the positions of the two mortises that hold the splat, then remove the bow and cut out the mortises to about $\frac{1}{2}$ in (12 mm) depth, offsetting them a little toward the back. Fit the bow over the splat and pull it down; mark the shoulders of the tenons on the splat, and trim them to fit. Draw around the underside of each tenon on the bow, then withdraw the bow and drill a small hole just below the mark, on the waste side, so that you can insert a thin nail to hold the tenon in place when gluing up.

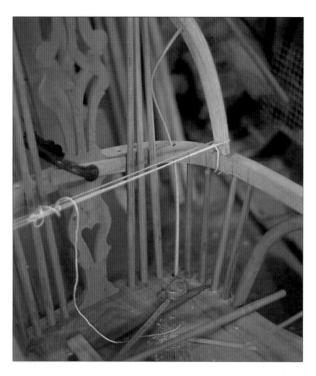

11 Mark the location of the sticks in the bow. Because each stick enters the bow at a different angle, poke a piece of quarter-round molding through the armrest into the seat holes, and mark off where the molding lies against the bow. Remove the bow, clamp it face up on the bench, and drill the holes to about $\frac{1}{2}$ in (12 mm) deep; angle the holes to suit both the lines on the front of the bow and the angle at which the sticks enter it, which is almost constant.

12 Reinsert the bow and hold it in place with thin nails through the tenon holes. Cut a thin offcut of flexible wood to a little longer than the longest stick, bend it into the armrest and seat and poke the other end into the bow. Trim the end until it fits snugly, then use this as a measure for the longest stick. Taper the stick to fit the holes in the armrest and bow, then number it before using the offcut to measure all the long sticks. Trim the ends so that the sticks slide into the holes easily.

13 Grease the locating nails for the armrest supports, then use them to glue and fit the supports. Glue the bottom ends of the short sticks and fit them to the seat, then glue the corresponding holes in the arm rest and drop it onto the short sticks. Place the temporary support under the armrest to keep it in position, and tap the arm rest onto the sticks.

14 Spread a little glue between the armrest and supports, and screw them tight. Glue the splat housings in the seat and arm rest, tap the splat gently into place, and clamp it up. Apply glue to the remaining stick holes in the seat and insert the long sticks, pulling them up about $\frac{1}{8}$ in (4 mm) from the bottom of the hole.

15 Apply glue to the stick holes in the bow and into the armrest mortises, then lower the bow slowly into position. For additional pressure, use a bar clamp against the top of the bow and a bearer stuck between the sticks at each side. With everything in place, slip the thin nails into the tenon holes in the bow, remove the clamp, and let dry completely. Trim the tenon ends and shape the armrest ends to finish.

Finishing

If you want to stain the chair, do this before gluing up. Bear in mind that oil-based stains are not compatible with epoxy resins (which are recommended because their slow drying time allows room for adjustment), so choose a water-based stain or one dissolved in denatured alcohol. Here, a light coat of aniline dye was applied to the whole chair, then a heavier coat was brushed onto the sticks, bows, stretchers, and legs, leaving the seat lighter to give

the impression of age. To achieve a traditional finish, apply two coats of button polish, rub them down and paint on the color variations using a finer brush and aniline dye. After sanding, apply another few coats of French polish, then sand once again and darken the areas around the back of the splat, under the armrest, and between the sticks. Finally, apply one more coat of polish, then wax the entire chair to finish.

LIST OF MATERIALS (*measurements indicate cut size*)

ITEM	SECTION	LENGTH
Hardwood/softwood for seat, 1	1ft 5½ in x 1½ in (445 x 38 mm)	1 ft 8 in (510 mm)
Hardwood/softwood for legs, 4	1¾ in (45 mm) diameter	6 ft 4 in (1940 mm)
Hardwood/softwood for side stretchers, 2, and center stretcher, 1	1⅛ in (30 mm) diameter	3 ft 10⅛ in (1169 mm)
Hardwood/softwood for splat, 1	5¼ x ⁷⁄₁₆ in (133 x 11 mm)	1 ft 11½ in (598 mm)
Hardwood/softwood for armrest bow, 1, and back bow, 1	1¼ x 1⅛ in (32 x 30 mm)	8 ft 2 in (2490 mm)
Hardwood/softwood for armrest supports, 2	1 x 1 in (25 x 25 mm)	2 ft 2 in (660 mm)
Hardwood/softwood for sticks, 16	⅝ in (15 mm) diameter	23 ft 8 in (7224 mm)

PINE BOOKCASE

This bookcase looks very good constructed from pine, but any softwood will serve the purpose. You can alter its dimensions to suit a specific space and add more adjustable shelves or support brackets.

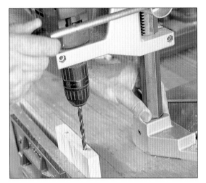

1 Mark and cut the sides to 3 ft 4¼ in (1021 mm) length, the top shelf to 2 ft 9⅜ in (850 mm), and the base to 3 ft ¾ in (933 mm). Plane the ends square. Mark the bottom ends of the sides and both ends of the shelf for dowel holes, and drill the holes using a ⁵⁄₁₆ in (8 mm) diameter bit.

2 Mark and cut a rounded shape to the front corners of the base. Using an ovolo roundover cutter in an inverted router, cut a rounded profile along the sides, corners, and front of the base. Cut a triple bead along the front edge of the top shelf.

3 Mark a line across the width of the base ⅝ in (15 mm) from each end, to leave ³⁄₁₆ in (4 mm) between the line and the beginning of the rounded profile. Insert brass dowel markers into the holes, and place the outside edge of each side against the line. Drill dowel holes in the base.

4 Cut the back top rail to 2 ft 11 in (890 mm). Cut a 2 in (50 mm) long, ¾-in (19-mm) deep notch on each top back edge. Drill screw holes in the top back rail to fit the notches. Cut a ½ x ½ in (12 x 12 mm) stopped rabbet along the inner back edges of the sides, the bottom front edge of the top back rail, and the top back edge of the base. Round off the top front corners of the sides, mark the position of the top shelf, then drill the dowel holes.

5 To set the bracket heights for the three adjustable shelves, make up a measuring stick with pencil marks for the heights along its length. Mark two points at each height on the inside face of each side. Use masking tape to set the depth for the bracket sleeves on a ¼ in (6 mm) drill bit, and drill out the holes to this depth.

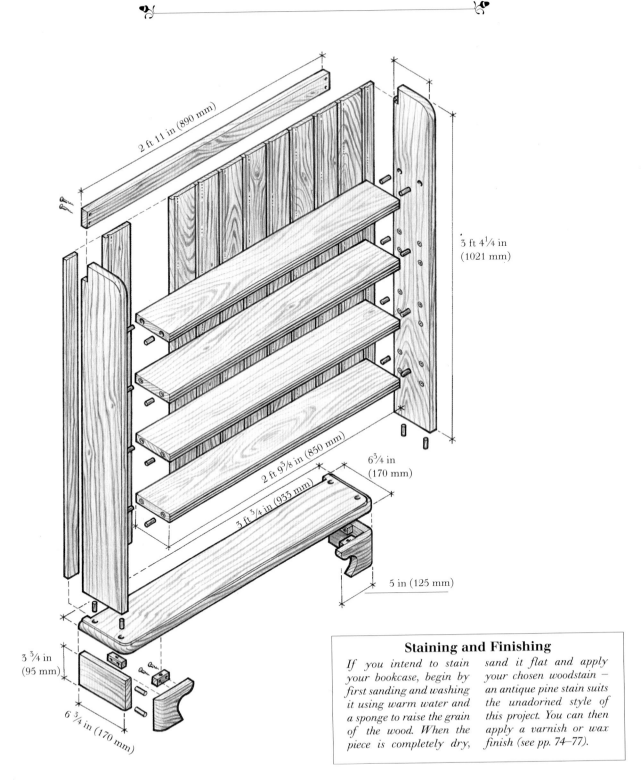

2 ft 11 in (890 mm)

3 ft 4¼ in (1021 mm)

6¾ in (170 mm)

2 ft 9⅜ in (850 mm)

3 ft ¾ in (933 mm)

5 in (125 mm)

3¾ in (95 mm)

6¾ in (170 mm)

Staining and Finishing

If you intend to stain your bookcase, begin by first sanding and washing it using warm water and a sponge to raise the grain of the wood. When the piece is completely dry, sand it flat and apply your chosen woodstain — an antique pine stain suits the unadorned style of this project. You can then apply a varnish or wax finish (see pp. 74–77).

6 Push the bracket sleeves into the holes and tap them into place with a medium-weight hammer. This project uses two possible heights for each shelf, but you can adapt the number of holes and their positions to suit your own needs. Dry-assemble the sides, top back rail, top shelf, and base, checking it for square.

7 Measure and cut the shelves to 2 ft 9⅜ in (850 mm), using the assembled carcass as a final measurement, then cut a triple bead along the front edges. Apply glue to the dowels and assemble and clamp the carcass. Mark and cut the bead and butt boards to 3 ft 2¾ in (985 mm) and drill each end with a ⅛ in (4 mm) bit, for screwing into the rabbets in the carcass.

8 Screw the boards to the rabbets. Cut the plinth fronts to 5 in (125 mm) and sides to 6¾ in (170 mm). Make up a template for the plinth shapes, and cut the shapes on the timber. Drill, dowel, and glue the plinths together, and round off the corners to match the base. Cut four glue blocks to 1⅝ in (40 mm), and use them to attach the plinths to the carcass, using glue and screws.

LIST OF MATERIALS (*measurements indicate cut size*)

ITEM	SECTION	LENGTH
Softwood for sides, 2	5¾ x ¾ in (145 x 19 mm)	6 ft 8½ in (2042 mm)
Softwood for shelves, 4	5⅛ x ¾ in (130 x 19 mm)	11 ft 1½ in (3400 mm)
Softwood for base, 1	6¾ x ¾ in (170 x 19 mm)	3 ft ¾ in (933 mm)
Softwood for back top rail, 1	2 x ¾ in (50 x 19 mm)	2 ft 11 in (890 mm)
Softwood for plinth fronts, 2, and sides, 2	3¾ x ¾ in (95 x 19 mm)	1 ft 11½ in (594 mm)
Softwood for glue blocks, 4	¾ x ¾ in (19 x 19 mm)	6½ in (160 mm)
Bead and butt boards, 10	3½ x ½ in (90 x 12 mm)	32 ft 3½ in (9830 mm)
Beech fluted dowels	5/16 in (8 mm) diameter	
Brass bracket sleeves, 24, and shelf supports, 12		
Dowel markers		
No. 8 woodscrews		1¼ in (32 mm)

CLASSIC MIRROR

This mirror has been designed for use with precut timber and moldings, which are available at most lumber yards and home improvement stores. All the measurements are approximate, and you may need to change them to suit a particular space.

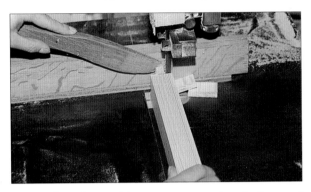

1 Cut 1⅜-in (35-mm) long tenons on each end of top and bottom rails, and 1½-in (38-mm) deep mortises at top and bottom of the 2 ft 2¼-in (665-mm) long upright sides. Use mortise-and-tenon or housing joints to fit the two rear 3 ft 9-in (1145-mm) long horizontal support rails to the upright sides, below the top rail and above the bottom rail. Rip 2¾ x ¾ in (70 x 19 mm) waste down the middle and fit it vertically between rails and support rails. Clean up faces that will be showing, and glue up and clamp frame.

2 Cut the two decorative moldings for the upright sides to 2 ft 2¼ in (665 mm) length and glue and fix them in place with very fine nails. Knock these away below the surface and fill the cavities; use a dark filler if you plan to use a dark finish, and a light filler for a natural finish. Mark and cut two 3 ft 9 in (1145 mm) lengths from 3¾ x ¾ in (95 x 19 mm), and glue and screw one to the bottom of the frame to form a shelf. Cut a 1 in (25 mm) strip from the other piece.

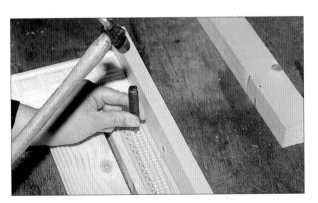

3 Glue and screw the 2¾ in (70 mm) section of the cut timber (bottom cornice support) to the top of the frame, and the 1 in (25 mm) piece (top cornice support) on top of it. Cut the two short returns, and glue and screw these into place. Cut the top rail molding to 3 ft 1 in (940 mm) and glue and nail it into place. Attach the glass plates to the top rail and bottom cornice support.

4 Cut three lengths of ¾ in (19 mm) waste wood and screw them to the top cornice support. Cut and miter the front cornice piece, using a miter box, with the longest ends at 3 ft 10⅜ in (1180 mm). Glue and screw the cornice front to the frame, using three screws, and drive fine panel nails into the back corner along the front edge (see inset).

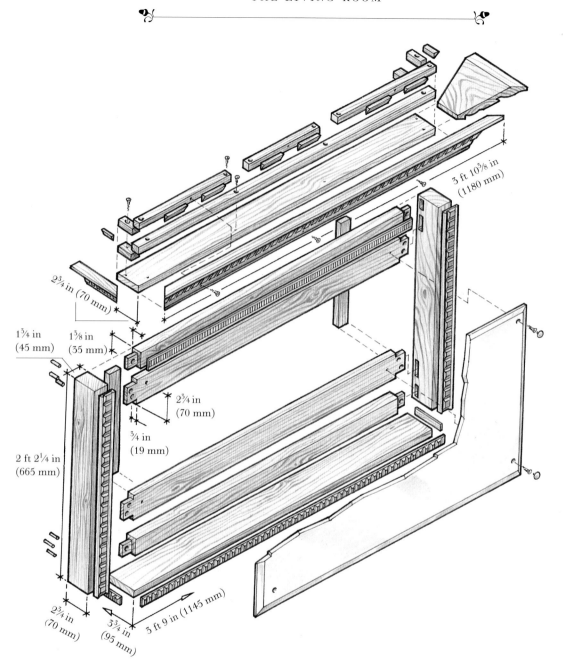

3 ft 10⅜ in
(1180 mm)

2¾ in (70 mm)

1¾ in
(45 mm)

1⅜ in
(35 mm)

2¾ in
(70 mm)

¾ in
(19 mm)

2 ft 2¼ in
(665 mm)

2¾ in
(70 mm)

3¾ in
(95 mm)

3 ft 9 in (1145 mm)

Finishing

This project can be stained or left natural, but be aware that if you decide to darken natural wood after assembly, the filler will always stay lighter than the wood. In this project, two coats of oak wood dye were applied to the surface, followed by three coats of antique pine sealer. Thin brushing wax was then applied because of its ability to reach every crevice of the moldings. The surface was buffed up and polished to finish.

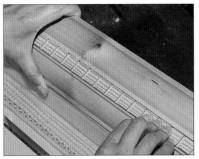

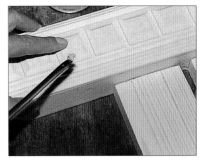

5 Cut six short lengths of angled section, supplied with the cornice, and glue these on either side of the screws. Cut and miter the two short side cornice pieces to 6 in (150 mm) at the longest, and fit them in place as for the front, again adding the angled section.

6 Cut the dentil molding for the sides of the cornice and the bottom shelf to length. Fix the molding in place with glue and nails as before, and then cut and fix the front pieces of the moldings.

7 Carefully examine the whole frame, filling any blemishes, nail holes, or marks. Sand and clean, then apply the chosen finish. Fit the mirror in place, following the instructions provided with it, without overtightening the screws.

LIST OF MATERIALS (*measurements indicate cut size*)

ITEM	SECTION	LENGTH
Softwood for top and bottom rails, 2	$1\frac{3}{4}$ x $1\frac{3}{8}$ in (45 x 35 mm)	7 ft 6 in (2290 mm)
Softwood for upright sides, 2	$2\frac{3}{4}$ x $1\frac{3}{4}$ in (70 x 45 mm)	4 ft $4\frac{1}{2}$ in (1330 mm)
Softwood for rear horizontal rails, 2, and bottom cornice support, 1	$2\frac{3}{4}$ x $\frac{3}{4}$ in (70 x 19 mm)	11 ft 3 in (3435 mm)
Softwood for shelf, 1	$3\frac{3}{4}$ x $\frac{3}{4}$ in (95 x 19 mm)	3 ft 9 in (1145 mm)
Softwood for top cornice support, 1	1 x $\frac{3}{4}$ in (25 x 19 mm)	3 ft 9 in (1145 mm)
Molded softwood for cornice, 1	4 x 3 in (100 x 75 mm)	4 ft $10\frac{3}{8}$ in (1485 mm)
Dentil molding for cornice, 1	$1\frac{5}{8}$ in (40 mm) wide	3 ft $7\frac{5}{8}$ in (1100 mm)
Decorative molding for shelf, 1	$\frac{3}{4}$ in (19 mm) wide	3 ft 9 in (1145 mm)
Decorative molding for top rail, 1	$1\frac{3}{4}$ in (45 mm) wide	3 ft 1 in (940 mm)
Decorative molding for upright sides, 2	2 in (50 mm)	4 ft $4\frac{1}{2}$ in (1330 mm)
Beveled mirror	2 ft $11\frac{3}{8}$ in x 1 ft $11\frac{5}{8}$ in (900 x 600 mm)	
Mirror fixing kit		
Glass plates, 2		
Woodscrews		
Fine wood nails		

WAX WORKS

Although wax finishing is easy, like some oil finishes it requires rubbing to produce a good result. It is quicker to achieve than a traditional oil finish, but it is not as hard-wearing. Prior to waxing, wood should be sealed to prevent dirt from penetrating the finish.

Carnauba wax
Harder than beeswax, in combination carnauba wax forms the basis for commercial wax polishes.

Commercial wax
Commercial wax polishes contain varying proportions of carnauba wax and beeswax.

Colored wax crayons
Wax crayons are precolored and can be used to fill deep scratches. Choose the color that best matches the original color of the wood.

Beeswax
The principal ingredient in wax finishes, beeswax is semi-hard at room temperature.

Types of Wax

The two main types of wax are beeswax, made from the comb of the honey bee, and carnauba wax, a vegetable product that is much harder than beeswax. Most commercial waxes are made from a mixture of the two in varying proportions, together with combinations of other waxes, such as paraffin wax and Japan wax. Some also contain petroleum solvent to make them dry more quickly.

Waxes that contain carnauba wax produce a harder surface that can be brought to a high gloss. Beeswax-only waxes can be a little sticky, especially if insufficient time is allowed between applications. Many wax polishes are available, but often manufacturers do not state exactly what their waxes contain, or in what proportions. Trial and error can be expensive, but you can make your own wax.

When to Wax

Because elbow grease is an essential element in wax polishing, it is best to wax inside surfaces before gluing up. Use masking tape to cover any areas to be glued up, as rubbing into corners does not give good results.

Grain filler is not normally used for a wax finish, as the polish tends to fill in the grain, but it can be used if you wish. You can also stain before waxing, but do not use an oil-based stain because it contains the same solvent as the wax; the stain will disappear from the wood as you apply the wax, resulting in a patchy appearance. For a total wax finish, use water- or alcohol-based stains.

Sealing Techniques

To prevent waxed surfaces becoming dirty with handling, you must seal the surface prior to waxing. You can use shellac sanding sealer, polyurethane, lacquer, French polish applied with a rubber, varnish thinned 10 percent with mineral spirits, or even Danish oil or teak oil, as long as these last two are left to harden. You can also use an oil-based stain on bare wood, as long as you seal it with shellac sanding sealer or French polish.

All sealers should be sanded lightly with old, worn 00-grade glasspaper before applying the wax. Apply the wax with a cloth and then rub it in with 0000-grade steel wool.

Sealing before waxing
Use fine steel wool to apply wax over shellac-based sealers.

Applying Wax

On flat surfaces, you can apply wax with either a shoe brush or a soft rag. A rag will help to spread wax that is quite hard in the tin; however, a stiff shoe brush is essential for waxing the finer crevices of carved wood. When you have finished applying the wax and it has hardened, use a clean shoe brush or a clean, soft rag to buff the surface.

The hardening time depends upon the ambient temperature, the humidity and the type of wax used. Always check that the wax is completely hardened – it should not be tacky to the touch – before applying another layer. Apply as many wax layers as you wish, remembering to test each layer for stickiness before proceeding.

Making Your Own Wax

To make enough polish to fill a 9 oz (250 g) tub, use 8 oz (225 g) of beeswax, $3\frac{1}{2}$ fl oz (100 ml) of pure turpentine, and three level teaspoons of carnauba wax; use bleached beeswax for a light-colored wax. This recipe will make quite a hard wax, producing a fast, high shine. For a softer wax, try 8 oz (225 g) of beeswax, $4\frac{1}{4}$ fl oz (120 ml) of pure turpentine, and a level teaspoon of carnauba; these waxes can be buffed up a few minutes after first application.

To make the wax, use a double boiler or two saucepans of different sizes. Put the water in the larger pan and bring to the boil. Place all the ingredients in the smaller pan and warm it in the boiling water, stirring with a wooden spoon until the wax has melted, or warm the turpentine and gradually add the wax, stirring until melted. Always remove the pan from the heat before adding ingredients.

Away from the heat, next add a small drop of mineral spirits to make the wax dry more quickly when used. Finally, pour into a suitable container and allow to cool. If you use a plastic container, make sure that it can withstand both the heat of the liquid and corrosive effect of the turpentine for long periods.

To create an antique effect, stir a little burnt umber and raw umber pigment into the molten wax. When set, the resultant polish has a gray-brown color, which gives a color cast like aged wood. When applying your antique wax, make sure that you allow it to accumulate in crevices and corners, where it can darken these areas.

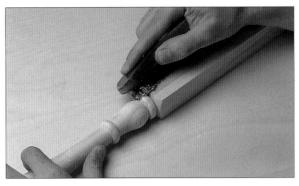

Applying wax with a brush
A stiff brush is the best tool for waxing carved work, keeping the recesses darker than the relief.

Making wax polish
You can make wax polish from beeswax, turpentine, and carnauba wax. Shredding the beeswax with a kitchen grater makes it finer and easier to blend when heated.

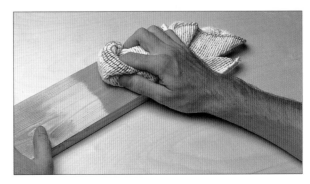

Staining with colored waxes
Colored waxes can be used to stain bare wood. Use for a complete finish by building up layers in the usual way. Alternatively, apply as a base color for layers of clear wax.

Making colored wax
Use a palette knife to mix pigment and neutral or clear wax. Combine 1 part pigment to 2 parts wax.

Applying colored wax
Apply the wax generously to the wood with fine steel wool, working it into the surface in all directions.

Removing excess wax
Use fresh steel wool to remove excess wax. For a deeper color, apply and remove more wax, working on one coat a day.

Using Colored Waxes

Colored waxes, or stain waxes, are used to stain bare wood surfaces. Proprietary colored waxes are available in a wide range of shades, and are useful for restoration work, making new carvings and furniture appear to have the patina of age. To achieve this effect, leave the wax thick in corners and recesses, making these parts much darker than the surface areas, which are buffed with a soft cloth.

You can also make your own colored wax, using pigments and clear or neutral wax. This means that you can make up as many colors as there are pigments, and can vary the strength of color to suit your requirements. The final color you achieve is also affected greatly by the color of the wood itself; timbers with a pronounced wood grain, such as oak, ash, chestnut, elm, pitch pine, and teak, work particularly well with colored wax.

Hot Waxing

Although less often used than other waxing techniques, hot waxing comes into its own in certain situations when you wish to create an immediate impression of age. Applying hot beeswax to stripped pine furniture or doors, for example, helps penetration and drives the wax deep into the surface, where it gives a yellowed finish. However, you have to work quickly, the molten wax can give off solvent fumes – so wear a respirator mask and work in a well-ventilated area – and a comparatively large amount of wax is used. The technique does not work on sealed wood.

Heat the wax in a double boiler until it is molten. Position the wood surface horizontally, then remove the liquid wax from the heat and brush it well out onto the wood; you do not need to cover the whole surface. Work quickly before the wax cools, and recharge the brush frequently. Allow the wax to cool for about an hour, then reheat small areas of wax with a hair dryer set to warm, not hot, and rub the heated area vigorously with a clean terrycloth towel, refolding the cloth regularly as it becomes clogged with wax. Go over the whole surface in this way until all the wood is burnished; apply cold wax periodically to maintain the finish.

Liming with Wax

Liming is a technique used to lighten the color of dark, open-grained wood, particularly oak, which gives a clean, country appearance to furniture. It was traditionally carried out by fuming the timber inside an airtight tent, but this is a cumbersome and potentially hazardous method, and the same effect can be obtained by applying white liming wax with fine steel wool. The alternative is to make your own liming wax, mixing zinc oxide with mineral spirits before mixing it into clear wax.

You can lime new or old surfaces, provided the timber is smooth and the surface pores are open. A greater contrast can be achieved if you stain the wood beforehand, but this must be thoroughly sealed with white French polish diluted by 50 percent with denatured alcohol, which allows the pores to remain open enough to accept the liming wax.

Wax Sticks

These sticks, sometimes referred to as beaumontage, are made from clear or colored wax to match most proprietary waxes, and are used in different ways for different results. One use is to fill minor blemishes in stripped furniture that is to be waxed, where other fillers may not make a good color match. The tang of a file is heated and held against the stick, and the molten wax is dripped into the blemish, and allowed to dry slightly raised above the surface. When it has hardened, the wax is levelled very carefully, using a sharp chisel.

Wax sticks and larger blocks, made of carnauba or a blend of carnauba and beeswax, are also used by wood-turners to polish their work on the lathe. The carnauba-and-beeswax blend is particularly useful for polishing wood with a soft texture, because it is less hard and brittle than pure carnauba, which can damage the work. With the work revolving at a slow speed, the stick is held against it, and the friction generated melts the wax. The stick or block is then slowly moved along the whole work; when it is covered, wood shavings are held against the wood to burnish it before the lathe is stopped and the work is buffed with a soft polishing cloth.

White liming wax

Phosphor bronze wire brush

Fine steel wool

Liming with wax
Rub a phosphor bronze wire brush hard along the grain to open it up, then apply white liming wax generously, across and then along the grain, using fine steel wool. Leave for a few minutes, but do not allow it to dry.

Removing excess liming wax
Rub all over the wood in both directions with a clean piece of steel wool, then use another fresh piece to apply clear or neutral wax. This ensures that the white remains only in the recessed grain.

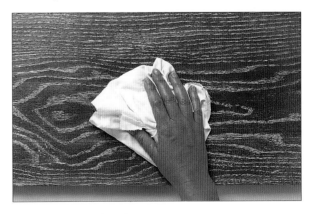

Finishing a limed surface
Use another piece of clean steel wool to remove the final traces of liming wax, and buff the surface to a soft sheen.

INDEX

A

aniline dye 65
antique finish 51, 75

B

bar clamps 7, 29, 32
beeswax 74, *74*, 75, 76, 77
belt sander 12, 23
bench vice 12
biscuit joiner 12, 32
bookcases
    Cherry Bookcase 6, 20–25, *20*
    Pine Bookcase 9, 66–69, *66*
brushing wax 72
button polish 51, 65

C

carnauba-and-beeswax blend 77
carnauba wax 74, *74*, 75, 77
CD Storage Rack 16–19, *16*
    CD holders, preformed 18, 19
    construction 17, 19
    dimensions 18
    materials 18
Cherry Bookcase 6, 20–25, *20*
    construction 21–22, 24
    dimensions 23
    materials 25
    sanding and finishing 23
chisels 7, 61
clamps
    bar clamps 7, 29, 32
    C-clamps 7
Classic Mirror 70–73, *70*
    construction 71, 73
    dimensions 72
    finishing 72
    materials 73

D

Danish oil 74
denatured alcohol 51, 65, 77
Double Display Shelf 7, 36–39, *36*
    construction 37, 39
    dimensions 38
    finishing 38
    materials 38
dovetail jig 29, 56
dovetail joints 29, 56
    half-blind dovetail joint *11*, 14
    through-dovetail joint 14
draw knife 63
Drawer Bench 52–57, *52*
    construction 53–54, 56
    dimensions 55
    finishing 57
    materials 57
drill 7

E

epoxy resins 65

F

filler 71, 72
finishing 7, 8–9
    antique finish 51, 75
    French polishing 51, 65, 74, 77
    liming 77, *77*
    oak 15, 33
    oil finish 23
    sealing the surface 74, *74*, 77
    wax finishing 9, 57, 74–77
    woodstaining 38, 57, 65, 68, 74
French polishing 51, 65, 74, 77

G

garnet polish 51
grain filler 74

H

hammer 7
hand tools 6, 7
hardwoods 8
hot waxing 76
housing joint 71

I

Inlaid Table 46–51, *46*
    construction 47, 49–50
    dimensions 48
    materials 51

J

Japan wax 74
jigsaw 7
joints
    dovetail joints *11*, 14, 29, 56
    housing joint 71
    lap joint *11*

K

knot sealer 45, 57
knots 45

L

lacquer 74
Ladies' Writing Desk 6, *8*, 10–15, *10–11*
    construction 12, 14
    dimensions 13
    finishing 15
    materials 15
liming 77, *77*
linseed oil 51
lumber yards 8

M

Mantelpiece 40–45, *40*
    construction 41, 43–45

dimensions 42
finishing 45
materials 45
marking devices 7
marking knife 7
marquetry 6, 49–50
masking tape 74
miter box 41
mitered tenons 53
moldings, precut 71
mortise gauge 7
mortise-and-tenon joint 27, 71

N
novice woodworker 7

O
Oak Coffee Table 30–35, *30–31*
construction 32, 34–35
dimensions 33
finishing 33
materials 35
oak, finishing 15, 33
orbital sander 12, 23
ovolo molding 14, 22, 29

P
paraffin wax 74
phosphor bronze wire brush 77, *77*
Pine Bookcase *9*, 66–69, *66*
construction 67, 69
dimensions 68
materials 69
staining and finishing 68
planes 7
polyurethane 74

R
reclaimed wood 27
roundover cutter 29, 56, 67
router 7, 17, 22, 53

S
sanders 7
belt sander 12, 23
orbital sander 12, 23
sandpapers 7, 23, 74
saws
coping saw 7
dovetail saw 7
miter saw 41
ripsaw 7, 17
tenon saw 7
scraper 23, 62
screwdrivers 7
sealing techniques 74, *74*, 77
shellac sanding sealer 33, 57, 74
Side Table 7, 26–29, *26*
construction 27, 29
dimensions 28
materials 28
softwoods 8
spokeshave 62, 63
steam-bending 60, 62
steel wool 33, 74, *74*, 76, 77, *77*

T
tables
Inlaid Table 46–51, *46*
Oak Coffee Table 30-35, *30–31*
Side Table 7, 26–29, *26*
teak oil 74
timber
hardwoods 8
purchasing 8
softwoods 8
tools 6–7
hand tools 6, 7
power tools 6–7
router 7, 17, 22, 53
sanders 7, 12, 23
saws 7, 17, 41
try square 7, 37, 39

V
varnish 38, 57, 74

W
wax finishing 9, 57, 74–77
applying wax 75, *75*
hot waxing 76
inside surfaces 74
liming with wax 77, *77*
oak 15, 33
removing excess wax 76, *76*
sealing before waxing 74, *74*, 77
wax sticks 74, *74*, 77
waxes
antique wax 75
beeswax 74, *74*, 75, 76, 77
brushing wax 72
carnauba wax 74, *74*, 75, 77
colored wax 74, *74*, *75*, 76, *76*
commercial wax polishes 74, *74*
Japan wax 74
making wax polish 75, *75*, 76, *76*
paraffin wax 74
wax crayons 74, *74*, 77
white liming wax 77, *77*
Windsor Armchair 6, 58–65, *58–59*
construction 61–65
dimensions 60
finishing 65
materials 65
steam-bending 60, 62
wood sealer 45
woodscrews
brass 15, 33
steel 33
woodstains 38, 57, 68
oil-based stains 65, 74
water- or alcohol-based
stains 65, 74
woodturning 6, 34, 62
workbench 7

ACKNOWLEDGMENTS

Makers

Mike Denley: Ladies' Writing Desk (p. 10), Pine Bookcase (p. 66),
Cherry Bookcase (p. 20), Oak Coffee Table (p. 30).
Peter Bishop: Mantelpiece (p. 40), Classic Mirror (p. 70),
CD Storage Rack (p. 16).
Bob Piper (Channel Rye Ltd): Drawer Bench (p. 52) and
steps for Side Table (p. 26).
James Wylde: Double Display Shelf (p. 36), and Side Table (p. 26).
Richard Jermy: Inlaid Table (p. 46).
George Buchanan: Windsor Armchair (p. 58).

Suppliers

Inlaid Table (p. 46): Mantelpiece courtesy of
Rudloe Stoneworks, Lower Rudloe Farm, Box, Wiltshire, UK SN13 0PB
Tel: (+44) 1225 811545 Fax: (+44) 1225 811343.
Side Table (p. 26) screen and cushions, Drawer Bench (cover, and p. 52):
courtesy of The Pier, London, UK.

Photographers

Sampson Lloyd: pp. 27, 29, 30, 40, 53–54, 56, 67, 69, 74–75.
Geoff Dann: Front cover and pp. 9, 20, 26, 36, 52, 66, 76–77.